The Bevin Boy

David Day

Ashford, Buchan & Enright

First published in 1975 by The Roundwood Press (Publishers) Limited,
Kineton, Warwick

This edition published by Ashford, Buchan & Enright
31 Bridge Street, Leatherhead, Surrey

ISBN 1 85253 286 6

Typeset by Priory Publications, Haywards Heath
Printed in Great Britain by FotoDirect Ltd., Brighton

Contents

50th Anniversary Foreword

By introducing the Bevin Boy scheme in December 1943 the Government was acknowledging the importance of the coal mining industry at that stage of the Second World War. To forego one conscript out of every ten available for armed service by directing him into civilian work was a recognition that the coal miner was as essential to the war effort as the soldier, sailor or airman. Looking back over 50 years one can see now that coal mining achieved its climax during the war and in the years immediately after. Since then the decline has been inexorable. At the time of the Bevin Boy scheme there were 1,570 collieries in Great Britain employing 709,000 people. By the beginning of the 1990s the figures had dropped to 54 collieries and 50,000 men. Many mining areas have changed out of recognition.

It is a disorientating experience to return to Wimblebury, the mining village where I spent all my time as a Bevin Boy. Our hostel has gone, of course, because it was never meant to last but so has the village, razed to the ground over 30 years ago, and so, now, has the colliery, which once dominated the valley, its buildings having been removed when drawing ceased to be economic. A place that was once as familiar to me as my native town no longer exists. Everything is changed.

When I wrote this book my intention was simply to describe my experiences as a Bevin Boy for a long three years and three months. I was unqualified to take a broader view. I had been as humble in the pit hierarchy as it was possible to be and had no knowledge of what went on at the colliery boardroom let alone at regional or national level. There were no Bevin Boy archives to consult and very little published material to read. All I could do was to write what I saw and what happened to me, but to do so I inevitably had to discuss the kind of jobs I was given and the conditions under which I worked and though I must not make too great a claim for this small book, I seem inadvertently to have recorded a form of underground life that has now gone for ever.

When I visited Chatterley Whitfield Mining Museum as one of a crowd not long ago and was taken below, I had difficulty in recognising the modern pit environment. Everything was metal, for example, all the roadways being lined with corrugated iron instead of wood as I remembered. When I commented on this our guide explained that this was because timber was regarded as a fire hazard. When I pointed out that there were no bell wires along the roadway - and every Bevin Boy will remember how we used to make a contact between the two wires to relay signals - the guide looked quizzical and said this was a bad practice which could spark an explosion and had long been done away with. It seemed strange to hear our days in the coal mines being spoken of as somehow primitive in the same way that we had regarded the previous generation's practices as being similarly archaic and dangerous. I must confess that I felt more at home when I visited the underground workings at the Black Country Museum where the intention has been to create a pit environment of the previous century.

With the passing of the old underground life, a whole vocabulary must have disappeared relating to timber alone. In our day, a roof support was known as a 'tree' and it supported a flat horizontal 'bar'. If there was a gap between the top of the tree and the bar, it was filled with a flat piece of wood known as a 'clet', and if further strengthening were needed, a small wedge called a 'timp', would be hammered in. Other small and useful bits of wood were a 'nubblin' and a 'sprag'. The roadways were lined from top to bottom with rough-edged planks, called 'slobs', smelling sweetly of the conifer trees from which they had been sliced. When timber had to be sawn off for size, the odd bits were sometimes smuggled out in the miners' bags and were known as 'cockwood'. In the innocence of youth I used this expression once in mixed company, causing the men to look sheepish and the women to chuckle and call me a naughty boy. I had not realised what might happen on the mat in front of the fire when a blaze of this purloined wood was emitting its seductive glow!

After cheating us of going into the forces by sending us down the mines, the Government appeared to lose interest in the Bevin Boys. There were no privileges apart from the extra soap ration allowed to all underground workers. There was not even a badge to wear in our lapels to show that we were doing our bit in a world where the man in uniform was king, and when the war was over and the method of release from the armed forces was announced, nothing was said about us until a campaign had been launched and we had enlisted the support of one or two sympathetic MPs. We were then told that we would be released at the same time as if we had been in the forces. "That is giving them almost favoured treatment," the Parliamentary Secretary to the Minister of Labour told the House of Commons. In what way "favoured", I wonder?

Those three years down the mines seem such a waste. Oh, I know the moralists tell us there is much of value to be learnt from our misfortunes, no matter how dire they may be, but I cannot believe that it is good for a youth's self-esteem to have to do a job, year in, year out, at which he is inept and ill-suited when all around him are doing their job extremely well! The years from 18 to 21 are recognised as being the most important of a person's life: the time when young people are acquiring that higher education and training on which their future careers will depend. I cannot think of a single skill I learnt in the mines that was of any use to me in my subsequent career though I had an unwelcome legacy for many years in the form of a recurring nightmare. If I happened to sleep flat on my back in bed, I would dream there was this heavy portmanteau rocking on a beam above my head and when it ultimately tumbled, I would leap from the bed to avoid it, taking all the bedclothes with me. Only a fool lies flat on his back in a coal mine where no roof is 100 per cent reliable.

If the scheme was intended as a social experiment it cannot have been a success. The parties involved just did not want to mix. I never went into a miner's home or made friends with a miner outside working hours nor did any of the other Bevin Boys of my acquaintance. There seemed a barrier between us, preserved as much on our side as on theirs, which only melted on neutral ground at the pub on a Saturday night when Bevin Boys and miners imbibed a mutual skinful of weak wartime beer. Presumably an influx of 20,900 ballotees, not to mention a further 15,700 optants, who had chosen mining in preference to the forces, must have boosted coal production though the full effect would have been diminished by rampant absenteeism. Having embarked on its foray into forced labour, the Government mitigated the force and paid the consequences in truant labour. No wonder it was eager to forget all about the Bevin Boys! Such a scheme is unlikely to be tried again.

DAVID DAY
Moreton-in-Marsh, 1993

CHAPTER ONE

The Letter

A T LAST IT was time for me to go upstairs and pack my things ready for the morning. I had put off this task for as long as I could but now I was glad of the opportunity to get away on my own for a while. My father and Mr and Mrs Bishop had given up trying to make conversation and we were sitting in a gloomy silence that made all four of us feel nervous and uncomfortable. As I closed the sitting-room door behind me I heard them resume talking, this time in whispers, and guessed they were back again on the subject they had so carefully avoided all evening: the subject of my departure the following day.

Upstairs I placed my small suitcase unopened on a chair, stretched myself out on the bed, relaxed and stared at the ceiling. Tomorrow I would be leaving home for the first time, an important step which every young man must take sooner or later, but now that my departure was no longer separated from me by a month, a week or any other comfortable period of time, and lay only a few hours distant, I realised quite plainly that I was afraid and did not want to go.

The irony of this was that hitherto my chief ambition had been to get away from Evesham, the small country town in which I had spent the entire eighteen years of my existence. The reason of course was that this was not the way I had planned it to be.

From where I was lying I could hear through the half-open window the noise of the river rushing over a weir only a short distance away. The river almost circles the town, wandering in from green fields and flowing under two shapely bridges before going off into the fields again. Sheltered by adjacent hills the town lies snugly within its river boundary, a picturesque collection of old houses grouped tightly round a tall bell tower, whose four gold-tipped weather-vanes, one on each corner pinnacle, glitter in the sunlight.

Earlier in the year the small town had been more full of people than at any other time in its indeterminate history. Every habitable building had been occupied by the military, British or

American, awaiting the D-Day invasion of Europe: all England was then like an armed camp, crammed with men and armour. D-Day had taken place in June, three months ago, and now the town was emptier and quieter than it had been at any time since the war started in 1939. The enemy bombers no longer throbbed overhead on clear nights, nor did the horizon light up with the awful glow of great fires where the distant industrial areas lay. There was a confident feeling everywhere that the war could not go on much longer.

The war began on my thirteenth birthday and at that time nobody imagined that I, then just a schoolboy, would ever be conscripted. A year later my mother died and for a time the events of the war were obscured by the shock of losing her: since her death my father and I had been zealously looked after by Mrs Bishop, who had moved into the country with her husband when their home on the South Coast had been bombed in one of the first air raids.

But five clangorous years of fighting had gone by; the schoolboy had grown up, and unexpected though it had seemed at one time his turn had come to go to war. In the spring of 1944 I reached the age of seventeen and a half and registered with my age group; after passing my medical examination I was interviewed by a recruiting officer who enrolled me for the army.

Nobody made bold prophecies any more about when the war would end because these had been disproved so often in the past, but the news was so improved that it seemed almost certain that by the time I had reached eighteen, entered the army and undergone my training, most of the fighting would be over and that I should never see the field of action. As it happened I was destined never to see the army either.

A cold draught of air crept in through the half-open window, making me shiver for it had a frosty bite in it. The summer had gone out like a bright lamp and the first month of autumn had almost run its course; the nights were drawing in and the morning air was sharper. Already my bedroom was getting dark, the familiar pattern of the wallpaper taking on fanciful new shapes in the trembling half-light. Outside everything was quiet and I could hear nothing but the weir and somewhere in the distance a dog barking vigorously.

It was on a summer's morning some weeks before my eighteenth birthday that the letter arrived: a morning on which I ought to have been up with the lark but which found me lying in bed long after most people had roused themselves, for I always found it easier to stay up late at night than get up early in the morning. (This was a point to count against me later on!)

As I hurried downstairs, just in time to prevent Mrs Bishop from clearing my breakfast away, I found a letter addressed to me, marked 'On His Majesty's Service'.

'It's not much good them calling you up when you can't get up in the morning,' said Mrs Bishop grimly, her eye on the O.H.M.S.

'They are not calling me up yet,' I said, quickly glancing through the contents of the letter. 'This is all about coal mining. They asked me when I registered whether I preferred to go into the mines instead of the Forces but I told them I wanted to go into the army. I saw an army officer and it was all settled. It was a waste of time their sending this to me.'

Whereupon I crumpled up the letter and threw it in the fireplace, then occupied by a fan of folded paper, its usual adornment during the summer when no fires were lighted. After hurrying through my breakfast I went off to work without giving the letter another thought.

Since leaving school I had been working in a local newspaper office: the war, the air raids and the uncertainties of the future having prevented me from taking a job farther afield as I would have wished. There was no difficulty in finding jobs in those days owing to the persistent staff shortage caused by men being called up into the Forces, though one had to learn quickly because it was not long before one's own turn came round to be conscripted.

Just as my predecessor had trained me to succeed him, so, as my eighteenth birthday approached, another youth was engaged for me to train to take over my work. It was rather like knocking the nails in one's own coffin.

When I returned home from work that day, Mrs Bishop was waiting at the gate to meet me. As I approached she drew out of her pocket a crumpled piece of paper and said, 'After you'd gone I picked up this letter and read it myself because I couldn't help feeling it was more important than you said.'

She added, significantly, 'I think you had better read it again. Last time you were in too much of a hurry to read it properly.'

Her manner was so ominous that without saying anything I went inside the house, smoothed out the letter on the table and read it again, this time more slowly. It was an insignificant slip of buff-coloured paper, thickly covered in small print on both sides and headed 'Ministry of Labour and National Service'.

'The Government has decided,' the letter began, 'that the essential manpower requirements of the coal mining industry should be met by making underground coal mining employment an alternative to service in the Armed Forces by directing to such employment a number of men who would otherwise be available for call-up for service in the Armed Forces. The method of selecting men for direction to this employment has been made public. It is by ballot and is strictly impartial. Your name is amongst those selected . . .'

Even at this second reading it was several moments before the full significance of this last sentence impinged on my brain. When it did I turned to Mrs Bishop, who was trying hard not to stare at me, and said in a tremulous voice, 'Do you realise what's happened?'

'Yes,' she replied 'they are sending you into the mines,' and she then burst into tears. I felt almost like doing the same.

Compulsory service in the coal mines had been introduced about a year before, the young men selected being known as 'Bevin Boys', after Ernest Bevin, the Minister of Labour responsible for the scheme.

Apparently every youth on registering was given a number ending in a digit from 0 to 9. Ten slips of paper, each bearing a single number, were placed in a hat by the Minister, who then called on one of his secretaries to make a draw. Every youth whose registration number ended with the number on the extracted piece of paper had to go into the mines whether he liked it or not.

It was an arbitrary scheme which ignored all niceties of background and education and it had been described as the biggest social shake-up in British history.

I had vaguely realised I was eligible for selection as a Bevin Boy but coal mining had seemed such a remote and utterly unsuitable occupation that I could not seriously imagine myself ever being thrust into it. Even now I found it hard to accept the Ministry's decision as final and anxiously resumed reading the letter, hoping to find some loophole by which I might escape.

'You may appeal against this notification,' the letter continued, 'if you consider that there are special circumstances connected with coal mining which would make it an exceptional hardship for you to be employed on that work.

'I have to remind you, however, that at the time of your medical examination under the National Service Acts, you had an opportunity of applying for postponement of liability to be called up under these Acts. If, therefore, you appeal against this notification, your appeal should show in what way you consider that employment in coal mining would be an exceptional hardship to you, having regard to the fact that either you made no application for postponement or that any such postponement has now expired . . .'

When my father came home and learnt the news he began to draw up an appeal, using such phrases in respect of myself as 'of an artistic nature' and 'totally unsuited to manual work', but I could see there were no genuine grounds for appeal and told him I must bow to the inevitable. If I was healthy enough to serve in the army there was nothing to prevent me from going into the mines.

The letter concluded 'Men are mainly required for *coalmining employment in Durham, Lancashire, the Midlands, Northumberland, Notts., Derby, Yorks., Scotland and Wales. No guarantee can be given of employment in any of these areas but individual preferences will be taken into account as far as possible. If you have a preference for employment in any of the areas indicated, you should write, even if you make an appeal against this notification, stating your preference and the address of any relatives or friends in a coal mining district with whom you could live'.

For several minutes our minds ranged over the family, pouncing on relatives near and far, but not a single one seemed to live in or anywhere near a coalfield, nor was there any friend, either on our side or on Mr and Mrs Bishop's with whom I could seek accommodation. I was clearly at the mercy of the Ministry and must go wherever they sent me. It was a gloomy quartet which sat down to a late meal that day!

During subsequent weeks, however, I derived a certain pleasure from observing the effect the news had on the various people I knew. If I had been given a stiff prison sentence they could not have been more perturbed. The majority had never seen a coal mine or been to a mining area and they had grim ideas of what working in such places must be like. The only cheerful response came from the young men with whom I had been at school and who were themselves expecting to go into the Forces at any moment. They just laughed their heads off at the prospect of me as a miner and said that coal output was sure to go down.

When I visited the Labour Exchange to fill in the inevitable forms the clerks treated me with unusual civility, for I was the first Bevin Boy the town had produced and dealing with me afforded them a novel exercise.

But such pleasures as I did enjoy from being the centre of so much interest and concern was obviously bound to be short-lived. A fortnight after my eighteenth birthday another letter arrived instructing me to report at a distant industrial city the following Monday morning for a month's training at a colliery specially adapted for training purposes.

The opportunity I had hoped for of getting out into the world and being independent had come at last though not in the way I had expected. In fact I would have given a great deal to be able to remain where I was.

My bedroom was now quite dark and I could scarcely see the pictures on the opposite wall or my small suitcase still lying unopened on the chair. For some minutes past I had heard Mrs Bishop moving about in the kitchen below and at any moment I expected her to call me down to supper. My oftpostponed packing would have to wait again until I came up to bed to spend my last night, for some weeks at least, under the family roof.

Fortunately I had very little to take with me. 'Bring two pairs of thick woollen socks, two shirts, (if possible, flannel), an old suit, two towels and an old mackintosh' said my instructions, and that was all.

On this last evening I could not help wondering whether anyone had ever found himself in such an absurd predicament as mine. There was I, who had never done any hard manual work in my life, being directed into the toughest industry in the country.

A good miner, I imagined, was short and stocky, but I was tall and thin; he used his hands and his muscle but I was notoriously clumsy and could not hit a nail in straight, let alone swing a shovel or a pick. I was quiet, inclined to daydream, as my school reports used to say: the last person, in fact, whom one would expect to fit satisfactorily into a coal mine. Only by a 'strictly impartial' ballot could such an unfortunate choice have been made!

When the expected call came from downstairs, I lifted myself off the bed and softly closed down the open window. Before drawing the black-out curtains I stood for a few moments, gazing out at the familiar hills and tree-tops darkly outlined against the night sky, and shivered at the thought of slag heaps on my horizon.

CHAPTER TWO

The Training Centre

THE NEXT MORNING I set off on the long railway journey to Coventry, the industrial city at which I was to undergo my month's training. As was usual in those days the trains were running well behind schedule and I arrived at my destination over an hour late. The railway platforms bustled with Service men and women in uniform, while overhead the smoke from locomotives seeped through large holes in the roof caused by air raids.

I had no difficulty in finding the office at which I had been told to report: it was a solid brick-built villa standing in one of the roads leading from the station. Obviously at one time it had been the home of a well-to-do family, and though now converted into Government offices it still had the look of a place where people had once lived leisurely and well.

On entering the front hall I was confronted by an astonishing collection of luggage, the tiled floor being littered with suit-cases, haversacks and bundles of all shapes and sizes. As these obviously belonged to other trainees reporting for duty that same morning I added my own suitcase to the collection, then looked around for someone from whom to seek instructions. A number of doors seemed to lead out of the hall and after knocking on two without producing any response I decided to wait until someone came along.

Standing alone in the deserted hall I began to study the various pieces of luggage, trying to build up a mental picture of what their owners were like, but after several minutes of useless conjecture I heard a number of masculine voices booming with laughter behind one of the doors on which I had not tried knocking. As there was still no sign of anyone coming into the hall I plucked up courage, grasped this door and slowly pushed it open.

'Ah, you must be the missing boy!' said a voice cheerfully. 'We wondered what had happened to you! Come inside and join the rest of your comrades!'

Through a fog of cigarette smoke I could see about thirty or forty young men seated round a small room, their faces turned towards me, and standing facing them in front of the fireplace a short jovial-looking man, to whom the voice belonged.

'I'm the welfare officer for Bevin Boys in this area,' he said to me, 'and I've just been telling the others what'll be happening to you during your month's training. I expect you'll pick up most of the details from the other chaps later. The important thing is that during your training you will be staying here in this city in a hostel built specially for Bevin Boys.'

He added that we would be expected to pay twenty five shillings a week for our board and that buses would take us to the colliery training centre at half past seven each morning.

With this he ceased to address me personally and resumed talking to the rest of the room, much to my relief for I had not relished being the centre of attention. I had tried to explain why I was late but neither the welfare officer nor the others seemed at all interested, and so I decided to keep quiet for the time being.

As all the chairs were taken I leaned myself up against a bookcase, trying to look more composed than I actually was: the others no longer stared at me though occasionally one would turn and give me a cold look. It was obvious I had not made a good first impression.

The rest of the welfare officer's talk was not intended to be instructive and consisted mostly of humorous stories about his job and about Bevin Boys during their first encounters with coal mining. His manner became increasingly light-hearted almost as though he was determined at all costs to put us at our ease, and I was reminded of a dentist humouring his patient before advancing on him for an extraction.

After making several more wisecracks, which set his audience booming with laughter again, he said, 'Well, I can't see much point in keeping you chaps here any longer. If you'll collect your things from the hall we'll make our way to the hostel. There's a bus stop at the end of the road from which we can catch a bus to the hostel. The fare is threepence, so please try and have the right money ready.'

On the way to the bus stop the welfare officer walked beside me, explaining some of the details I had missed, but my mind was too confused to take in all that he said. This business of catching a bus to the hostel and paying twenty five shillings a week for our board had completely thrown out of perspective my conception of life as a Bevin Boy.

I had imagined we would be like soldiers without uniform, subject to the same rigours, discipline and occasional privileges, but instead of being taken off to some camp in special lorries here we were, standing in the same queue as a straggle of housewives, waiting to be taken on a threepenny bus ride to a hostel apparently run on civilian lines, where we would have to pay twenty five shillings a week for the privilege of staying.

During subsequent weeks it became apparent that we were in fact ordinary civilians like everyone else, the only difference being that we were doing a job that had been thrust upon us. This obviously had its advantages. It meant, for instance, that once we had done our day's work we were free to do just as we pleased, but it also had its disadvantages: principally that we had no uniform or other means of identification to indicate that we were doing our bit as ordained by the Ministry of Labour.

The result was that we were curtly treated by many people, such as shop assistants or bus conductresses, who made it pretty clear that they thought we were shirkers, and waitresses in tea rooms invariably made us wait longer than was either polite or necessary.

On board the bus I tried chatting to the young man on the seat next to mine, but his replies were terse and clearly not intended to be friendly. Most of my comrades, as the welfare officer had called them, seemed to know each other, and I discovered later that they were nearly all 'optants' who had chosen coal mining in preference to the Forces and who came from roughly the same part of the country.

Their reason for choosing coal mining was that they lived in or near a coal mining area, and once they had finished their month's training they intended to live at home or at least travel home each weekend. They kept tightly to their own chummy group, making me feel unwanted and an outsider.

The hostel stood in one of the city suburbs called Keresley, on a large patch of open ground surrounded by rows of modern houses. It consisted of several blocks of semi-circular roofed Nissen huts, and from the outside looked like a rash of green fungus that had sprung up during the night.

Inside however the contrast was immediate. The walls were painted in bright colours and the layout resembled that of a seaside holiday camp. The main block, or welfare block as it was called, boasted among its amenities a shop, a cinema, a games room with billiard and table tennis tables, a library, a vast dining hall and a well upholstered lounge.

The dormitory blocks were not so good. Each room had six lockers and narrow beds on either side, with a hot water pipe running round the ceiling and heavy black-out curtains drooping at the windows. I had been given a bed number but had not met the other occupants of my dormitory.

After seeing that we were enrolled into the hostel and issued with meal tickets, two for each day, breakfast and evening meal, the welfare officer took his leave of us.

'I hope you chaps will be comfortable here,' he said cheerfully. 'I don't suppose any of you are looking forward to being coal miners but try and make the best of it. By helping to produce more coal you'll be doing a worthwhile job for the war effort besides learning a lot that you didn't know before. And, don't forget, if any of you run into trouble or need any advice I shall always be glad to help you!'

With a friendly smile and wave of his arm he then sailed out of the entrance hall, and I never saw him again.

A large blackboard in the hall proclaimed in coloured chalk that in the evening there would be a talk by a member of the hostel staff on 'How to do card tricks'. As I had nothing else to do I decided to go along, hoping to make some friends there, but only six other people attended and they were all members of the staff. However the talk helped to pass an awkward evening away, though I could not help wondering where all the other new trainees had got to.

At half past nine the dormitory was deserted, and as I was determined not to be the first in bed I went back to the welfare block and wrote a couple of letters, chiefly in order to kill time.

Six return visits during the next hour and a half found the dormitory as empty as ever; at last my determination faltered and I got into bed. By this late hour I was becoming anxious about my ability to get up at half past six the following morning.

I had scarcely put my head on the pillow when the door burst open with a bang and my eleven dormitory mates tramped in. They had all been drinking, and though the noise they made was enough to waken the dead I decided it advisable to look as though I was sleeping through it all.

With my eyes tightly shut I could hear them gathering round my bed, the beery smell of their breath wafting over my pillow.

'Shall we tip him out and see if he's got fancy pyjamas on?' said one of them in a threatening voice that made me tremble under the bedclothes.

A good deal of laughing and muttering went on before another voice replied less aggressively, 'No, let him rest tonight. There'll be plenty of other nights to find that out!'

To my relief they then disbanded and went to their own beds, but showed no inclination to get between the sheets. For some time they lay fully clothed on top of their beds, exchanging jokes, but eventually they undressed and got into bed, without putting out the lights. Their night attire consisted either of their underwear or old shirts they had brought for the purpose.

It was about midnight then and I was beginning to despair of getting up in the morning, but the revelry had only just begun, the next hour being spent in community singing: old songs, new songs, sad songs, happy songs, sentimental songs and filthy songs, emerging from apparently inexhaustible repertoires.

When at last their voices died down and one by one they sank off heavily to sleep, I took the opportunity to wriggle out, of my pyjamas and kick them secretly to the bottom of the bed. It was the last time I wore them for the rest of that month!

In the morning I was awakened by what was to become a very familiar and unwelcome sound: the clinking of black-out curtains as they were drawn back by the nightwatchman.

'Wake up me lucky lads!' he said. 'Six o'clock!'

I felt as though I had only been sleeping a few minutes. I dashed some cold water in my face in the ablutions but I still felt pretty numb. After a dismal breakfast I hurried off with the others to board the bus waiting outside to take us to the colliery.

It was a twelve mile journey to the colliery along wet roads lined with doleful elms. For most of the way we were in open country, where autumn had the landscape firmly in its grip. The grass beneath the trees was thick with brown leaves; puddles spotted the empty fields and lazy mists rose from the hollows.

The appearance of Haunchwood colliery, the first I had ever seen, was quite different from the grim mental picture I had formed beforehand. It lay at the base of a steep valley surrounded by wholesome pastures, where cattle grazed serenely in the autumn haze. Apart from the colliery and its appendages the scenery was green and unspoilt, even the slag heaps being smothered with soft grass and frothy masses of seeding willowherb.

Another time I might have regretted that this pleasant valley, so much like the countryside at home, had been marred by the intrusion of a coal mine but on this particular morning I could not help feeling cheered to be starting my career as a miner in such a familiar and reassuring setting.

There were already three groups of trainees at the colliery with either one, two or three weeks training behind them, and as we newcomers arrived they lined the banks, showering us with boos, catcalls and abuse. Apparently this was a tradition of the training centre and a week later we did the same thing when the next batch of trainees arrived.

On reporting at the pithead we were issued with overalls, pit boots and safety helmet, and given an identity number: mine was 111, which was easy to remember. We were told by the senior training officer that each day during our training would be divided into three periods, consisting of lectures, physical training and surface or underground work. Our wages during training would be £2. 10s.0d. per week from which stoppages would be made for baths and bus fares.

After these preliminaries we went off to our first lecture, which was followed by P.T. This accounted for the morning, and after a midday meal in the pit canteen we spent the afternoon on surface work, unloading timber from railway wagons. It was all very dull.

Although used as a training centre the colliery was still engaged on full-scale coal production, the timber we unloaded being destined for pit props underground. Occasionally I saw a man with a blackened face walking from the pithead and, imagining him to have just returned from the depths, gazed at him with awe and hero worship. He was probably only doing one of the dirty jobs on the surface but I wasn't to know that.

We were not due to go underground ourselves until the following week, and though most of us found the prospect intimidating we hoped it would be more interesting than the surface work had been.

Once the first day was over the rest of the week quickly went by and I soon found myself falling into the daily routine along with the rest of them. Owing to my former lay-a-bed habits I usually had to race through breakfast to catch the bus, but somehow I always made it.

The twenty minute ride to the colliery provided a good excuse for a sing-song, even at half past seven in the morning, and the small villages along the route used to echo with chanting voices as the Bevin Boys' buses roared through their quiet streets.

One of the songs was a sad ditty sung, as follows, to the tune of 'Broken Doll':

As I walked down the street the other day,
A damsel turned to me and she did say:
'Why aren't you in khaki or navy blue
And fighting for your country like the other boys do?'
I turned to her and this I did reply
The answer nearly made the poor girl cry!
'The army I have tried to join
But Bevin sent me down the mine
And left me with a broken heart!'

Most of the other songs were unrepeatable.

The daily periods of physical training took place either indoors at the miners' community centre or out of doors on the colliery playing field. The indoor P.T. included vaulting exercises which I regarded as a danger to wind and limb; however, we had to queue up in a long line to take our turn and by continually shifting my position towards the back of the queue I was able to prevent my turn from ever coming round.

The outdoor P.T. consisted of ball games. During the first week we had football matches wearing our steel toecapped pit boots, but there were so many casualties due to unscrupulous shin tapping that the boots had to be abandoned in favour of gym shoes. After taking one or two hard swipes with these, one used to try and avoid rather than go after the ball.

The lectures on the other hand were quiet restful occasions. As they were given with the aid of lantern slides the room was blacked out for this purpose. With restricted ventilation and the all-inviting darkness it was not long before the class was dozing, though the lecturer always drew the line at snoring. Under these conditions very little knowledge of coal mining was acquired, though I was grateful that the sleep inevitably lost at night could be regained for a short period during the day.

The surface work, which after the first week came on alternate days with the underground work, was the worst part of the training. Our chief task was either loading or unloading railway wagons, a monotonous job that made the time pass very slowly. The weather was often cold or wet and this added to our frustration.

Despite ourselves we began to grow impatient for our first descent underground, especially after the more experienced trainees had told us it wasn't so bad when you got down there. The colliery had two shafts, one of which was in regular use for coal drawing. The other, which descended to a non-productive area of the pit, was the one used by the trainees. Both shafts were of course surmounted by the familiar outline of the pit-head wheel and the winding gear, which lowered and raised the cages.

When the time came for us to go below we took it in turns to pile into the narrow metal cage, everyone on board wearing an apprehensive look. We had heard it was customary for new trainees to be given an extra rapid descent on their first cage run, as a form of initiation, and after making the trip I could well believe it.

A pit cage drops enormously faster than a lift in a shop or hotel. The first seconds are the worst with your stomach gyrating and the wind roaring up your trouser legs as the cage hurtles downwards. By the time you have reached the bottom your eardrums seem to have caved in, but this feeling is remedied by pinching your nose and blowing hard.

Though this first cage run left us breathless it was amusing to see the startled faces of those coming down on the next run.

Any misgivings that we might have had about going underground were soon dispelled once we got there. With helmets on our heads and lamps in our hands we felt almost as though we were embarking on some boyish adventure. The roadways were all broad and reasonably high, though to my surprise they extended for miles and frequently went up and down steep gradients. In my ignorance I had imagined that all the tunnels in a coal mine were flat!

It was in these roadways that most of our subsequent training took place. We were taught how to couple coal tubs together; how to clip a line of tubs to a moving rope so that they were transported to their destination; and how to give signals to stop or start the rope. Sometimes we went to a heading: that is a place where a new roadway was being excavated through the rock, but our training was mostly concerned with haulage procedure. It was pretty clear that after leaving the training centre most of the Bevin Boys were expected to be working in the haulage roads and not on the actual coal face.

All the instructors underground were ex-miners who had volunteered for the job, not, I suspected, without a certain amount of leg-pulling from their former colleagues. After several months at the training centre they had become extremely wary of Bevin Boys, none more so than Dad, a hard-bitten old collier whose demeanour struck fear into the heart of the most intrepid trainee.

It was true that some of the Bevin Boys were difficult to handle, especially those who came from mining areas. They were proud of the fact that hitherto they had avoided going into coal mining, which they regarded as a degrading occupation, and were determined that everyone should know they did not accept their present enforced entry into the pits willingly or with good grace. Their attitude towards the instructors and other pit officials was deliberately provocative.

Old Dad was well aware of this, and having a fair sized chip on the shoulder himself he delighted in taking us down a peg if the opportunity presented itself. The following typical incident occurred during one of his instruction periods.

'Well, how would you lads set about drawing out this piece of timber?' he said, indicating a projecting spar on the side of one of the haulage roads then under repair.

No reply came from the trainees.

'Can't any of you say anything?' Dad grumbled.

'You come down 'ere pretending you've got all the brains and that all the miners is a lot of ignorant pigs! Make a sergestion if you can do naught else!'

One of the trainees then bravely suggested how he thought the timber should be removed, this being immediately followed by a snarl from Dad.

'Well, I've been down the pit all my life,' he said, 'and I'm damned if I've ever heard a sillier sergestion! Why, man, you'd have half the roof down on your head before you was finished! If you lads can't think o' nuthin better than that to say, you might just as well keep your mouths shut!'

And that's how he'd go on.

The irony of our training was that we never saw any coal nor did we ever get dirty enough to have to take a daily shower in the pithead baths. The coal drawing areas of the pit were all centred round the other shaft, where loaded tubs were speeding upwards to the surface at a rhythmic pace throughout the day.

Our training accustomed us to going underground, but as far as practical experience of coal mining was concerned we were as ignorant at the end of the month as we had been at the beginning.

At the hostel I led a solitary existence. I used to spend most evenings writing letters home, going to the pictures or walking the streets, always alone. My dormitory mates seemed to regard me as a sort of curiosity: if I addressed one of them it was a signal for the others to stop talking and stare at me as if amazed that I had a tongue. At first this isolation worried me; then I grew indifferent, and at the end of three weeks I could still say I hadn't a friend in the place. I vowed that if given the choice I would never stay in a hostel again.

Round about this time we were notified that on completing our month's training we would be posted to a colliery to start work in earnest as coal miners. Those of us who had not stated a preference for a particular area, when first directed into the mines, were all destined for the large coal mining district known as Cannock Chase.

When I was asked – somewhat unnecessarily, because I did not know the district – to state at which Cannock colliery I wished to work, I automatically chose the one which offered accommodation in private houses as an alternative to hostel life. All the others who were not going to live at home chose to go to a hostel but I had no regrets about my decision.

Each Saturday morning saw an emptying of the hostel as everyone packed bags and went home for the weekend. Only a handful of trainees stayed behind, including myself: my home was too far away for a worthwhile weekend visit and anyway I felt I could not face so soon all those people to whom I had bidden a dramatic farewell only a short time before.

On Saturday nights, when I had the dormitory to myself, I was able to enjoy a long unbroken sleep, the only night of the week when this was possible. How I hated Sunday nights when the others returned and the rumpus of the first night was re-lived all over again!

The undoubted leader of the dormitory was a thickset young man with a toothless mouth, sallow face and hair like damp straw. His leadership appeared to result from his beer-drinking proficiency and his pugnacious manner towards those who displeased him. His nickname was Cag.

A favourite trick of his was to kick the legs from under beds so that their occupants, who were then lying at an angle of forty five degrees, with the top end of the bed standing normally and the bottom end resting on the floor, slid helplessly down the mattress under the sheets. Most of us in the dormitory fell victim to this trick, myself in particular, though no one thought it wise to remonstrate in any way.

A weekly custom that must have caused a headache for the hostel management was the Friday night farewell celebration held by the group of trainees completing their month's training. This celebration usually took the form of a drinking session at the local pub from which the participants returned to the hostel ready for anything. The result was smashed windows, beds and fittings in the morning.

I had watched with growing anxiety the noisy departure of three groups, and as my own group's last week of training drew to a close I could not help wondering what form their farewell celebration would take. From the occasional glances that Cag gave me I suspected he was not going to let me escape from his clutches scot free. My fears were not allayed by an incident which occurred a couple of nights before our final night in the hostel.

My dormitory mates came in just after closing time, no more intoxicated than usual but in an ominously quiet mood. I noticed that one of the party was missing and heard mumblings about someone dodging his round. When the missing lad came in no one spoke and the atmosphere was as tense as the lull before a thunderstorm.

Softly they undressed; the lights were put out and everybody got into bed. Nothing happened for a few minutes: then I heard feet padding down the dormitory floor. This was followed by the crash of a bed collapsing, a howl and the sound of blows. Suddenly all the lights went on, and peering over the sheets I could see Cag attacking the boy who hadn't paid his round.

The latter, whose bed was a wreck, bore up well at first but when the others joined in against him the odds became too great, and with blood running from his nose he flung open the door and raced crying down the corridor. The others climbed back into bed with the air of those who had seen justice well and truly done and peace settled over the dormitory once again.

In the morning, as we were getting dressed, the door opened and a light-haired young man, whom I recognised as a fellow trainee occupying one of the other dormitories, came in.

He gave the impression of being a tremendously strong person. His shoulders were broad, his hands big, and his features crudely yet pleasantly cut. He looked like a boxer, which was in fact what he proved to be. But though his appearance was powerful his manner was neither aggressive nor intimidating; his voice was quiet and his gaze simple and direct. He was the sort of man you would instinctively trust on sight.

He walked slowly up to Cag, looked him straight in the eye and said firmly, 'I reckon you know what I've come about, Cag. I've just heard what happened in this dormitory last night, and I'm telling you straight, I don't like what you and your mates done to that chap. You never gave him a chance.'

'Aw, come off it, Jack,' said Cag, showing his gums ingratiatingly, though not without effort. 'It ain't no business of your'n.'

'When you and your mates sets about a bloke I makes it my business,' replied Jack sternly. 'What you done last night was dirty. If you want to scrap, why don't you do it man to man? I'm warning you, Cag, if you tries anything like it again, you'll have me to reckon with!'

The rest of the dormitory awaited Cag's reaction, half expecting a brawl, but apparently the visitor was too tough a proposition for our leader.

'All right, Jack,' he said, his smile drooping. 'I can take a hint. But I don't see what you'm making all the fuss about.'

Jack did not argue the point. He gave Cag a final glare, looked warningly at the rest of us, then left the dormitory.

'Bastard!' hissed Cag, as the door closed to, but my own feelings were that Jack was a hero.

I could not help wishing that a month ago I had been allocated a bed in his dormitory, where I was sure the nights were peaceful and secure.

When our last Friday at the hostel arrived the others were full of what they were going to do at that night's farewell celebration. I tried to console myself that if any trouble came my way Jack would be within shouting distance, but I realised I could not be sure he would come to my rescue or even that he would hear me. Any retribution he might exact the following morning would not be much help to me then. I decided there was only one thing for me to do.

Plucking up courage I went up to Cag, who was talking to the others, and said, 'Do you think I could come along with the rest of you tonight?'

He looked amazed. 'But you ain't a drinking man,' he said. (This was fairly obvious since I had only reached the permitted age of eighteen a few weeks before).

'Well, I've got to start some time,' I replied, feeling bolder, so I might as well start tonight. Where shall I meet you?' For a moment Cag hesitated. He obviously did not want me to come but in a way he was just as curious about me as I was afraid of him. At last his curiosity got the better of him.

'Okay,' he said, 'come along if you want to. We're meeting at seven o'clock.' And he gave me the name of the pub.

I thanked him and went off to my breakfast.

Our last full day at the training centre went by uneventfully; it ended with our saying goodbye to the instructors and handing in our gear, though we were allowed to retain our pit helmets and boots. All that we had to do the following, Saturday, morning was to present ourselves at the colliery in our ordinary walking-out clothes and sign off.

I felt extremely nervous as the evening approached. Not only was it the first time I had been out with my dormitory mates: it was also the first time I had taken part in a drinking session. As I washed my face and brushed my hair in the ablutions I prayed that nothing would go wrong and that I would not make a fool of myself in front of the others.

The pub they had chosen was not the large modern one near the hostel. It was an old-fashioned building standing in a quiet side street where my footsteps sounded loudly as I walked along the damp pavement. Inside however it was a friendly cheerful place; thick black-out curtains shut out the wet night; a warm fire burned in the grate and the well polished furniture shone like a new pin.

My dormitory mates were all there, except for the victim of the previous night's episode, and they were obviously quite at home, joking among each other and with the genial landlord behind the bar. It appeared they had made the pub their regular rendezvous during the past weeks, much to their own and to the landlord's satisfaction. No other trainees were present. They were presumably doing their celebrating at one of the more obvious pubs elsewhere.

I was given a friendlier welcome than I had expected, which soon dispelled my shyness. It was decided that we should all put seven and sixpence in the kitty instead of taking it in turns to buy rounds, and from then onwards the polished table top in front of me saw a succession of shiny pint glasses filled with frothy brown liquid.

My relationship with the others might have been strained at first but by eight o'clock I was feeling they weren't such bad fellows after all; by nine I was convinced they were the best bunch of chaps in the world, and by ten I was hanging round their necks, singing the same silly songs I had despised before.

An extra subscription was made by each of us to the kitty, but by the time the number of pints per person had reached double figures the landlord was calling 'Time' and we reluctantly had to go.

We linked arms together and danced a grotesque palais glide back to the hostel, thundering our way into the welfare block where by a fortunate coincidence a dance was then in progress. Pushing our way past the stewards we poured into the hall, and continued to dance uninhibitedly until one by one we were hustled out and sent packing to the dormitory.

I was the last into bed that night. I walked down the dormitory nonchalantly, kicked the legs from under Cag's bed, which fell to the floor with a crash, and then collapsed and passed out on my bed.

The next morning I did not breakfast alone. The others called me to their table and told me to sit down with them. Apparently I had done better than expected at my beer-drinking initiation the night before and they now regarded me as one of themselves. I was happy to be on such friendly terms with them after being on my own for so long though of course it was all too late.

A few hours later, after signing off at the training centre, we stood in the centre of the city saying goodbye before going on our various ways to catch trains and buses home. As the others were going to live either at home or in a hostel it seemed unlikely that I would ever see any of them again.

'I only just get to know you and we have to split up again,' I said somewhat emotionally to these eleventh hour friends of mine.

'Well, it's your own fault!' retorted Cag, raising his voice over the traffic's roar. 'You could have had yourself a good time, if you hadn't been so bloody stuck up in the first place!'

CHAPTER THREE

The Bank

ON THE FOLLOWING Monday morning I set off by train
again, this time bound for Cannock Chase, the coal mining
area in Staffordshire to which I had been directed from the
training centre. It was there that I would have to begin in earnest
my career as a coal miner though I did not deceive myself by
supposing that I knew a great deal more about mining than I had
done a month before.

As the train approached Cannock I got my first glimpse of the
Chase, a hilly plateau rising bleakly from the lowland, its slopes
striped with the dark green bands of conifer plantations.

Before entering Cannock the train went past several small
collieries, each surrounded by rows of drab brick houses, where
presumably the colliery workers lived. These housing rows
pushed outwards from the colliery, then ended irresolutely in
open fields. The area appeared to be a large unplanned sprawl,
consisting not of one large centre but of a multitude of little
communities, each gathered round its own pithead.

On arriving at Cannock, a small busy town, I reported to the
Labour Exchange and was given a note of introduction to present
at the colliery. As already stated, I had been allowed to choose
the colliery at which I wished to work and had chosen the one
which offered private accommodation as an alternative to living
in a hostel. This was Littleton Colliery, apparently the biggest and
deepest in the area, and though my views on hostel life had since
changed considerably I did not unduly regret having chosen to
go into private digs.

To reach the colliery I travelled from Cannock on a
double-decker bus which lumbered uphill for about two miles till
it reached the top of the rise from which I had my first
unforgettable view of the place where I was to work. The Chase
at this point dropped gently to the flat lowland, and where the two
met, there lay Littleton Colliery.

It covered an enormous area with four pyramidal slag heaps,
the largest I had ever seen, rising in the background like grey

volcanoes. A mechanical tipper scurried up and down the slopes of one of the slag heaps like an insect, emptying its load on the summit before descending the near vertical track for further supplies. In the foreground were two tall chimneys ringed with metal bands and belching out a black smoke that contrasted with the white clouds puffing up from the locomotives below.

A sea of railway tracks lapped up against the brick colliery building where the gaunt towers of the pithead stood out sharply against the sky, their wheels spinning blurrily as the cages raced up and down. On the tracks wagons loaded with coal were shunted to and fro on the first stage of their outward journey from the colliery while others stood in sidings piled high with brown timber, waiting to be unloaded.

At the colliery offices I presented myself to the Pit Welfare Officer, an amiable man who explained that for the first fortnight I would be working on the surface and not underground. My rate of pay during this period would be £3 per week and the hours would be from 7 a.m. until 3.30 p.m. When I went underground my pay would be £3. 10s. and the hours from 7.50 a.m. to 3 p.m. I was to start work the next morning at seven and he gave me the name of the surface foreman to report to.

Next came the question of accommodation. Most of the houses nearby were owned by the colliery and let to its employees, who had been asked to put their names on a list if they were prepared to offer accommodation to Bevin Boys. He gave me half a dozen addresses off this list and advised me to see whether I could get fixed up at one of them.

The first two houses on my list looked uninviting and so I gave them a miss. At the third the lady said she had changed her mind, while at the fourth a group of grubby children answered the door so I changed my mind! At the fifth a soldier, obviously home on leave, slammed the door in my face, and behind drawn curtains proceeded to harangue his missus for putting her name on the list in the first place. At the sixth there was no one at home.

I was getting worried when I returned to the Pit Welfare Officer for more addresses.

Stroking his chin he said, 'There's a Bevin Boy hostel at Wimblebury, about four miles from here. I don't know whether you can get from there each morning, but if you could get fixed up at the hostel for the time being, we could meanwhile look around for some permanent accommodation for you here.' After what I had seen that morning the thought of living in a hostel held no fears for me and I eagerly took the next bus to Cannock en route for Wimblebury, which was located right in the heart of the mining area.

The first person I saw in the town was none other than my old dormitory leader, Cag, and I was never so glad to see anyone in my life. It was just after closing time and he had obviously been drinking. Apparently Wimblebury Hostel was the place to which he and many of the others were going and so we travelled together, he enlivening the bus journey with loud gibes against Mr Bevin, the Bevin Boy scheme and mining in general.

The hostel lay in a bleak valley, the fields surrounding it rising gradually till they merged with the heather and bracken of windswept moorland. A road as straight as an arrow's flight divided the valley into equal halves, sweeping from one hillside to the hollow, then up again to the opposite rim. Sharing the hollow with the hostel, though separated from it by the road, was Wimblebury Pit, a smaller one than Littleton and appearing much more so from the hill above.

On the slope above the pit stood Wimblebury village, several slummy terraces with brick walls, slate roofs and innumerable smoking chimneys. It looked like some drab corner of the city dug up by a giant spade and capriciously deposited in the green of the countryside. All the houses stared down at the pit as if mesmerised by its presence: the gaunt chapel was one of the few buildings to look the other way.

The bus did not descend into the valley but continued along the outer rim: therefore Cag and I dismounted at the top of the straight road and walked down to the hostel. Both inside and out it was identical in design with the hostel at which we had stayed during our training, though the jumble of green Nissen hut roofs seemed to fit more naturally into a semi-rural setting than it had done in the town.

I rejoiced to find that a number of the lads from the training centre, whom I had never expected to see again, were already in residence, though when it came to moving into a dormitory I made sure I did not go into the same one as Cag. I saw very little of him after this and a few weeks later he left the hostel for good after a disagreement with the management.

Recalling his fearless conduct at the previous hostel I seized the opportunity to move into the same dormitory as Jack the boxer, who was another new arrival, and we soon became friends though our relationship began in a rather unusual way.

To keep in training he used to spend much time prancing up and down the dormitory, shadow boxing. One evening he had his imaginary opponent cornered up against the door and was just about to finish him off with an uppercut when the door opened, I walked in and fist met jaw. The result was a perfect knock-out! When I came to I was lying on the bed with Jack pouring water in my face, apologising profusely and offering to let me take a swipe at him. Just to please him I accepted his offer though I'm afraid the blow was a disappointment to him. Afterwards we became the best of friends.

The hostel had only been open a few months and still smelled of fresh paint and furniture polish. The dormitory occupied by Jack and me had never been used before: it was exactly like the dormitories at the other hostel with six beds and lockers down each side. One of the first things we did was to chalk in big letters on our locker doors the time at which we wished to be called in the morning by the nightwatchman, who began calling up at five a.m.

There was accommodation for five hundred residents at the hostel, but though I was No. 461 on the books I was the first resident to work at Littleton Colliery. However, after making inquiries I found it was possible to get to Littleton each morning, a bus leaving from the top of the road at 6.16.

On my first evening I called at the local pub, my beer-drinking initiation having quickly got me into the habit, and sat brooding over a half pint in the smoke room. The only other person present was an elderly lady sipping a glass of stout.

Edging towards me she said, 'Are you one of them Bevin Boys?' I replied that I was.

'Such a shame 1' she said, 'sending lads like you into the pits what isn't used to it. Where are you staying?' I told her I was at the hostel.

'Oh!' she exclaimed 'they never do you proper in them places! It's not like being in a real home! If ever you gets fed up with it and wants a change, you're welcome to lodge at my house. My husband was a collier for thirty years before he died so I know what it's like to look after someone what works in the pits.'

Whereupon she gave me her name and address.

After thanking her and saying goodnight, I left the pub feeling fortified by the knowledge that whatever happened to me in the future I always had a place of refuge to run to.

The next morning I was roused by the nightwatchman at five thirty and leapt out of bed with an alacrity that amazed me and dashed off to my breakfast. On the way to the colliery I got on and off the wrong bus several times but eventually arrived at my destination with about a quarter of an hour to spare.

The first place I made for was the pithead baths, a modern building that supplied the miner's every need from rotating mechanical brushes to clean his boots to a de luxe glass-walled canteen. The building had two floors, I being on the first floor.

Each man had two lockers: one for his clean clothes and the other for his pit clothes, the clean lockers being located in one half of the building and the dirty lockers in the other. The procedure in the morning was to undress and put your clean clothes in your clean locker: then walk through the building to your dirty locker, where you put on your working clothes. At the end of the shift the procedure was reversed, the only difference being that after taking off your working clothes you went under a shower before returning to your clean locker.

The lockers were in two tiers – I had an upper one – and formed ten enclosures, each occupied by about twenty people. I shared my section with a remarkable assortment of miners. In the corner was an ill-tempered elderly man, covered from head to foot with tattoo decorations, who made a point of shoving past you without ever a smile or word of pardon. Immediately below me was a short middle aged man on whose bald head I was terrified of dropping my pit boots; and next to me on the upper tier was a quiet shy boy who had just left school. In another corner was a strapping curly-haired young man who looked too sunburnt to be a miner. I discovered that he too was a Bevin Boy though he travelled from home each day and did not live in a hostel. He was called Curly.

For my working clothes I had brought an old navy suit of my father's and in this and my helmet and pit boots I felt ready for anything. It was dark and the stars were still shining when I reported to the Surface Foreman. I had been told to ask for Ern Brown, and though I felt embarrassed at my familiar use of his name – where I had come from all my superiors were either Mr or Sir – he did not seem to mind and took me into his office, where a warm fire was burning.

He told me that although I had to report at seven, work did not start until half an hour later when all the men were down below and the pit began 'drawing'. In the meantime he advised me to get thoroughly warm before the fire.

Just before the pit siren blew half past seven he patted me on the shoulder and said, 'Hadn't you better go and put your working clothes on?'

'But these are my working clothes,' I said.

'Crumbs!' he exclaimed in a shocked voice, 'they look better than what I wear on Sundays!'

At the first opportunity I got hold of some dirt and tried to smear most of this Sunday look away.

There were two drawing shafts at Littleton Colliery, No.2 and No. 3, No. 1 having been flooded many years before. No. 3 was the downcast shaft, down which travelled the fresh air supplying the pit, and No. 2 was the upcast, up which came the spent air after its journey below. The top of No. 2 shaft was enclosed by an airlock to prevent the inrush of fresh air and to facilitate the escape of the foul air; and it was in this airlock that I was put to work.

The cage raced up and down the shaft every few seconds, bringing up six loaded tubs, three on a deck. The top of the shaft was enclosed by wooden doors and as the two banksmen, as they were called, lifted up these doors and pulled off the tubs of coal, it was my job to stop the tubs from bumping through the outer doors of the airlock until the shaft doors had been closed again. I did this either by sticking a 'scotch' in front of the wheels or a 'locker' inside them, or simply by hanging on to the tubs like grim death.

After the shaft doors had been closed, I had to push the six tubs through the outer doors as quickly as possible so that the banksmen could reopen the shaft doors when the cage returned to the surface again. As the outer doors burst open there was a sudden inrush of air and all the loose slack in the tubs swirled up, blackening my face and blinding my eyes.

It was a loathsome job. The full tubs were partly pushed off the cage by empty ones shoved on from the opposite side and as the two lots came together the din was terrific. The routine was maintained without a break, hour after hour, the cage racing up and down the shaft with tireless speed. At the training centre I never saw any coal. Now I was both inhaling and digesting it.

At eleven thirty it was lunchtime, or 'snapping' as it was called, and I went over to the canteen for a cup of tea. Being unaware that we were only allowed a quarter of an hour break during the shift, I became alarmed on noticing about half an hour later that I was sitting alone in the canteen. I hurried back towards No. 2 shaft and was within a short distance of it when I heard a voice shouting behind me. I turned to face the Under Manager, who was hurrying towards me, red-faced and obviously very annoyed.

'What the hell do you think you're doing?' he bellowed at me. 'Quarter of an hour is your snap time, not half the bloody morning!'

Before I could attempt to explain he went on, heatedly, 'I've just about had enough of you lot! You're more confounded trouble than you're worth! You come here knowing nothing about the job and lounge about as though you own the bloody place! You're bone idle, the whole damn pack of you! Believe me, if I get any more trouble from you, my friend, you'll find yourself chucked out on your ear! Now get back to your blasted job and stay there!'

I felt shattered by his outburst, which was not the sort of reproof to which I had been accustomed. It was pretty obvious that the Under Manager did not like Bevin Boys, and it also turned out to be the beginning of a long personal feud.

The ironic part of course was that he knew and I knew that there was no question of throwing me out on my ear. The colliery was stuck with me and would have to put up with me. Herein lay one of the principal defects of the Bevin Boy scheme.

If a Bevin Boy failed to work properly what was to be done with him? If he was sacked he would have to be transferred to another colliery where presumably he would behave just as badly. The only real answer was to send him into the Forces, which was probably just what he had wanted in the first place.

Introducing Bevin Boys into the pits was a bad blunder in this respect. Miners who had been willing to knuckle under in the past were not so inclined to do so after seeing Bevin Boys cheek the gaffers and get away with it. In fact I doubt whether pit discipline was ever the same again.

This news of only a quarter of an hour's break came as a shock to one who had always been accustomed to an hour's break in the middle of the day and the rest of the shift seemed awfully long in consequence. It was a great relief when it was over and I could bathe in the showers and wash the filthiness away.

Taking a daily shower was the best thing in coal mining. It meant that every afternoon you walked from the pit, feeling fresher and cleaner: almost that the day was beginning all over again, but in the evening, when you blew your nose, there were tell-tale marks on your handkerchief and coal dust kept gathering in the corners of your eyes and darkening your lashes like mascara. After a day or two the inside of your underwear turned black from coal working out of your pores even though you were taking a shower every day.

During the next fortnight the weather grew much colder, but the pithead on these frosty December mornings was a magical sight with the rail track lit by glowing braziers and the dark sky overhead shining with stars. As the underground men walked from the lamphouse to the shaft the scene glittered with hundreds of moving handlamps while in the background loomed the slag heaps, showered with embers and sparkling like mountains of jewels.

There was no further comment from the Pit Welfare Officer about the permanent accommodation he was going to find me while I was temporarily fixed up at Wimblebury, which was just as well because I was soon happily settled in at the hostel. I had mastered the system of travelling to and from the pit each day and found I could buy cheap return tickets, which made it quite inexpensive.

I remained on my job in the airlock for the entire fortnight, disliking it more every day. The only opportunity I had of talking to my workmates was at snapping, and since this was over almost as soon as it had started I did not get to know them very well.

One morning the news flashed over the Bank – it was no longer the 'surface' – that they were bringing up a badly injured man from No. 3 Pit and at snapping we stood in solemn groups watching the stretcher carried by.

'That's another one from the Shallow,' Ern Brown said to me. 'They all come from the Shallow. Don't let 'em send you there when you go down.' But at that moment I didn't care where they sent me so long as it was away from the airlock!

CHAPTER FOUR

The South Shallow

AT THE END Of my first fortnight at Littleton Colliery I finished working on the Bank and reported to the Under Manager for underground employment. He entered my name in the underground workers' register and gave me a lamp and check number, 170. He told me that I would be working down No. 3 Pit and that for the first fortnight I would be in the pit bottom, the area immediately surrounding the base of the shaft.

At the check office I collected my check, an oval piece of metal stamped with the number 170, which was used as a check on all men working below. If at the end of a shift a man's check was not handed in, it was presumed he was still down below. It was not an infallible system however. On a number of occasions I forgot to hand in my check and went home with it in my pocket but I never heard of any search being conducted for me below.

I then collected my pit lamp from the lamphouse. This was done by shouting my number through an open hatch whereupon an attendant collected the lamp from its appropriate bracket number and handed it out to me. It was a heavy clumsy object with a large hook on top which served as a handle to carry it by. All the miners walked with their lamps hanging gracefully from their belts but I couldn't do this without it cracking against my knees, so I carried it by hand.

At the pithead I joined a long queue of miners waiting to go below. Underground men were urged to come early in order to avoid queuing but most of them preferred to stay in the canteen for as long as they could. If you missed the last cage descent at half past seven you were unlucky, there being no special trip for latecomers. After getting up early, travelling to work and changing into your working clothes, it was a frustrating thing to happen.

Travelling on the cage was in some respects like travelling on a bus. A banksman counted you on, and if too many boarded the cage he would not give the lowering signal until some of the riders had come off. Even so we were generally tightly packed. On this

31

first morning I felt lost, jammed in the middle of about twenty miners, their clothes smelling of coal dust, sweat and tobacco.

Littleton Pit was deeper than the pit at the training centre and the cage seemed to drop with greater speed. I don't think I ever got used to this early morning drop. I used to think of it as the black minute when everything became dark and noisy as the cage roared downwards, and my fear of the rope breaking never quite went until the lights of the pit bottom had come into view.

The pit bottom must have been about fifteen feet high with white-washed walls and bright roof lights, which made hand lamps unnecessary. Stretching away on one side, almost as far as the eye could see, was the main haulage road with journeys of full tubs coming towards the shaft and empty ones travelling away from it. On the other side of the shaft the road ended abruptly, forming a short 'dead end'.

I soon found that my new job was just a variation on my previous one. When all the men had descended the cage commenced its rapid journeys up and down the shaft, taking up the full tubs and bringing down the empty ones. The empty tubs on the cage were shoved off by full tubs from the main haulage road and ran on to points on the 'dead end' side of the shaft.

It was my job to turn the tubs on these points and couple them together so that they were facing the main haulage road, ready to move off in that direction. When about twenty tubs had been coupled together a man attached the front tub to a moving rope and in this way the whole journey moved forward, going past the side of the shaft into the main haulage road.

Most of the haulage in the main roads was carried out by means of a steel rope travelling between the tub tracks at ground level. By clipping journeys of tubs on to a moving rope it was possible to convey them to their destination without a great deal of supervision except at certain checkpoints. Bevin Boys quickly learnt how to clip and unclip tubs to a moving rope and were widely employed in the haulage roads.

After a few hours at my new job I felt like a robot, pushing tubs, twisting tubs and coupling tubs. The cage kept racing up and down the shaft, never letting up for a minute, and the only break during the shift was a quarter of an hour for snapping. As this was the downcast shaft there was a continuous breeze from the incoming air and it was bitterly cold. I worked with my jacket on and some of the others had scarves and overcoats as well. At least

I kept clean: so clean that it was unnecessary for me to have a shower at the end of the shift.

An ill-omened incident occurred soon after snapping on my first day below. There is a right way and a wrong way of coupling tubs together and the wrong way is to get your finger inside the hook as you couple it on to the link. This was what I was doing when the man in front of the journey fastened the tubs to the moving rope and jerked them into motion.

My finger suddenly went numb. At first I dared not look at it; then I felt blood trickling into my palm and saw that the skin round the centre nail had been torn off. One of the men saw me trying to bandage my finger with a handkerchief and told me I could get it dressed properly at an ambulance station in the main haulage road.

The ambulance station proved to be nothing more than a tool house with a First Aid box inside. It had been cut out of the rock and its interior looked very much like that of a shed in the garden. A fat bustling man was working in the road and when I told him about my finger he said, 'I'll soon fix you up, my lad. I know all about First Aid.'

He looked at the finger. 'H'm,' he said, 'better make sure there's no dirt in the wound,' and with reassuring confidence he uncorked a water bottle and proceeded to empty its icy contents like a miniature Niagara over my bleeding finger.

The dancing spots in front of my eyes became all enveloping darkness and I collapsed to the ground. The next thing I heard was a voice shrieking, 'Bill! Come quickly, for God's sake, Bill!' and when I came to, there was my First Aid friend shaking like a leaf and saturating my shirt in his attempts to pour water down my throat.

With the arrival of Bill he calmed down a little and the two of them lifted me to my feet prior to jerking my head between my legs several times until I was back to normal. They then bandaged up the finger.

When told what had happened Bill shook his head and said to me sadly, 'You'll never make a pit man.'

'I'm hanged if I want to!' I retorted, and stalked back to my job, humiliated at such a bad start to my underground career.

At the end of a fortnight I was told to report to the underground office, a neat little chamber cut out of the rock, with a high sloping desk, ledgers and ink wells. It was the headquarters of the Overmen, who were in charge of the various districts in the pit and next in authority under the Under Manager. One of them entered my name in his ledger and said 'I'm sending you to the South Shallow. Report to the District Fireman. He'll tell you what to do.'

Ern Brown's warning about the Shallow was forgotten in the excitement I felt to be escaping from the monotony and clangour of the pit bottom, and without a moment's hesitation I started walking down the main haulage road away from the shaft.

Fifty yards from the pit bottom, on the left hand side, was a turning where the District Firemen used to assemble in order to avoid the full draught of the downcast air as it whistled along the main haulage road.

Each man working in the pit had to report first thing to the District Fireman, who not only told him where to work but also kept a record of the number of shifts and overtime he put in. It was advisable to keep on good terms with your District Fireman because if he liked you he'd see that you had a good job, and if he didn't he'd either give you a bad one or refuse to have you in his district.

It was also the duty of the District Fireman to see that the men in his district did not carry cigarettes, matches or other inflammables. This involved searching the men when they reported for duty though it was not often done, the men realising it was in their own interest not to bring down anything that was likely to cause a fire or an explosion.

After entering me in his register the District Fireman of the South Shallow searched me, presumably because I was a newcomer: then told me to go along the middle road, past the loader, and start work with Levi.

The plan of the South Shallow resembled a giant capital E with the vertical stroke representing the two hundred yard length of the coal face, and the horizontal strokes the three roads leading to it from the main haulage road. These three roads were known as the top, middle and bottom roads, the middle one being the most important because it contained the loader over which passed all the coal drawn from the face.

The South Shallow was quite near to the pit bottom, the turning in which the District Fireman stood being the entrance to the top road: so by proceeding down the main haulage road I reached a second turning on the left which was the middle road.

As I entered this road, I left behind the roof lights of the main haulage road and stepped into darkness lit only by the lamp I carried. I had never really appreciated it until then.

The middle road was a typical pit road: a semi-circular tunnel consisting of arched girders, roofed in with flat wooden boards known as 'slobs.' Cut into the side of the road at regular intervals were manholes, where haulage workers could take refuge in the event of tubs running amok or some other disaster. On ground level were two simple tub tracks with moving ropes, one taking the empty tubs in and the other bringing the full ones out. As yet however the ropes and tubs were stationary, the shift not having officially begun.

I walked down the middle road for about half a mile till I reached the loader, where a number of men were squatting down waiting for the rope to start. I asked them where I could find Levi but none of them took any notice of me apart from scowling, as if to say 'What the hell will they send down next!'

Then a voice said, 'I'll take you to him, mate,' and emerging from the shadows I saw Curly, the Bevin Boy with whom I shared my section of the baths. He was a dark, good-looking fellow, only two or three years older than myself and invariably had a grin on his face. 'Follow me, mate,' he said cheerfully, 'I'll show you the way.'

At the loader the conveyor belt from the face was suspended several feet above the ground so that empty tubs could be pushed under the end of it to catch the coal as it cascaded off. When the tubs were full they were coupled together, clipped on to the moving rope and dispatched to the pit bottom. The moving rope and double tub track ended at the loader: from here onwards all supplies for the face were carted along a single tub track by pit pony.

Curly led me past the loader in the direction of the face. The road now became lower; the metal arches were distorted out of shape by the weight above; broken slobs projected dangerously and minor falls of rock blocked the tub track here and there. Curly told me that this was only a temporary road: as the face advanced it would be replaced by a larger better road, such as existed prior to the loader. It became very much warmer too, and perspiration began to drip from my forehead.

The floor of the road was covered with thick grey dust, composed of a mixture of coal and stone dust. It was a common sight down the pit to see men transforming the roadways white by throwing stone dust everywhere, like sowers scattering seed. By diluting the coal dust the risk of combustion was reduced.

As we tramped along, one behind the other, Curly told me he had been working on the loader for several weeks.

'What have you been doing, mate?' he asked me over his shoulder.

I told him I had only just come out of the pit bottom.

'In that case you'll find it better working in the Shallow,' he said, adding 'Head', meaning that I should duck to avoid a projecting slob. 'For one thing, it's warmer. Head. And we get a longer snap provided the gaffers aren't about. Feet', meaning that I should beware of tripping over a lump on the track.

'Of course, it's further from the shaft,' he said, 'which means we can't get up so quickly at the end of the shift. Feet. But if the face draws off early we stand a good chance of getting to the pit bottom within ten minutes of knocking-off time. Head. That's quicker than you can do it from most other districts.'

After a short distance, when our two lamps were the only lights to be seen in the dark, Curly told me to sit down and we squatted side by side on the rubbery conveyor belt, which was now at its normal level about two feet from the ground. With his eyes glittering in the dim light Curly went on, 'What you've got to remember, mate, is that it's no use letting these blokes get the better of you. Your life won't be worth living if you do! You see, they know all about this job and we don't, so it's easy for them to take advantage of you if you let them. An inexperienced lad like yourself is just the sort they'll pick on. I know because they tried it on me when I first came down the pit. If they start trying to push you around you've got to stand up to them and tell 'em you're not having it, get me? They won't think any the worse of you if you do.'

Gratified by his interest in my welfare I thanked him and said I understood, which was not entirely true (though I was to understand later on), whereupon he gave me a friendly slap on the back and said, 'Okay, then. That lesson's over. Now let's get moving again.'

As we advanced towards the face a cluster of pinpricks of light glittered before us like distant stars. These lights slowly grew larger till I could see they were handlamps festooned over the roof and walls of the road like lanterns at a ball. A few yards beyond the lights the road ended abruptly in a solid wall pierced by a low gaping hole, the entrance to the face. Curly and I had come along the road just about as far as we could go.

Sitting in the glow of the lamps were about twenty or more men quietly eating sandwiches. It was the custom among miners to have something to eat before starting the shift though I never felt like anything myself. With sudden awe I realised that these were none other than the facemen, the key workers of the pit around whom all the elaborate machinery above and below ground was built and on whose efforts the prosperity of the colliery depended; the men who worked stripped in the heat and dust digging the coal from the earth, and at this time of the year when the days were short rarely saw the sunlight.

Curly was the first to speak. 'This is a new lad,' he said, pointing to me. 'He's been told to work with Levi.' Then turning to me, he muttered, 'I've got to go now. The loader will be starting soon. Take care of yourself and don't forget what I told you!' With a farewell grin he then hurried off in the direction of the loader, leaving me alone with the facemen.

They were not big men though they had a tough sinewy look. What struck me most about them was their whiteness. They were not sunburnt like Curly or me and in the dull glow of the lamps their faces seemed to have been moulded from colourless wax. Only their eyes were dark and alive. Despite the fact that down a pit your head is the most vulnerable part of your body, few of the facemen wore helmets but had tight fitting berets or skull caps, cut from old trilbies or discarded hats belonging to their wives.

After looking me up and down for several moments, they asked me my name and where I came from.

When I had told them one of the older men said to me, 'Well, what do you think of working down the pits?'

'Not much,' I replied.

'Ha!' he said. 'I don't suppose you do but wait till you've had about forty years of it!'

This remark created a chuckle all round.

Then a small thin man with a genial face interposed, 'You know, it don't seem right to send an educated lad like him into the pits. They 'adn't ought to have picked on lads what wasn't used to it and didn't know aught about the job.'

At first this was received with murmurs of approval by the others, who continued to study me in between biting into their sandwiches, but suddenly a sharp-eyed man with taut cheek-bones cut in bitterly, 'And why not? Is he privileged or something? Why shouldn't people like him come into the pits and get a taste of what it's like? They're always ready to criticise the miners. Scum of the earth, they call us! Well, let 'em come and see what the miners have to put up with!'

'This lad, here,' he said, gesturing towards me. 'All his life he's been burning coal in the grate. Did he ever think of the blokes what had to get it? No! He didn't give a damn about us! The miners wasn't good enough for him! Well, now he's down the pit himself! Let him see whether he enjoys being a miner! Let him see whether coal is worth the price!'

This outburst met with an enthusiastic uproarious response, and a debate broke out in which fortunately I was quickly forgotten. I retreated into the shadows, feeling half scared and half ashamed since there had been a certain amount of truth in what he said. The debate however was destined to be shortlived, for only a few moments later the lifeless conveyor belt leapt into motion like a wakened serpent. The day's shift had begun.

One by one the facemen grabbed their lamps and went off in the direction of the face, taking their picks and shovels with them until there was only one person left: a wiry old man, aged about sixty, with deeply lined features. This was my workmate, Levi.

'When you come down the road with Curly,' he explained, 'you saw how bad it was in places. There're slobs sticking out and parts of the side have fallen in. We've got to patch it up and tidy it up as best we can till they're ready to make a better road of it. It shouldn't be a bad job for the two of us.'

Working with Levi was very different from anything I had known on the Bank or in the pit bottom, nor was there any question of my being imposed on in the way Curly had suggested.

When we reached a spot where the wall of the road had partly fallen, causing a heap of débris, I got hold of my shovel and started digging furiously to clear up the mess.

Levi looked shattered. 'What are you moitherin' yourself like that for?' he asked in a shocked voice.

'Well, it's got to be shifted, hasn't it?' I replied.

Levi looked at me pityingly. 'Come here, lad,' he said. 'I want a word with you. Get yer a minute.'

So we both squatted down beside the tub track.

'Now we've got a nice little job here, haven't we?' he explained, 'and when you've got a nice little job down the pit you tries to make it last as long as you can. Get me? If you go at it bull-headed and finish it off, no one will thank you for it and you'll have done yourself out of a good job. So let's take it steady, eh? As long as the gaffers always catch us working we shall be all right.'

My week with Levi was the pleasantest I had experienced since I became a Bevin Boy. Every so often he'd growl, 'Get yer a minute!' and we'd both stretch out, always making sure of course that we had a safe bit of roof to relax under. He had been in the pits ever since he was a lad and told me many tales of when he was a young man in the bad old days. He had served his time on the coal face and was now employed on light work.

Naturally one of us had to keep an eye open for gaffers. This was not difficult because approaching lights could be seen from a long distance and the gaffers' lamps were easily recognisable. All the ordinary pit workers carried heavy wet cell lamps which gave off a dull adequate glow. Gaffers on the other hand carried 'shinies': lightweight dry cell lamps with brilliant flashing beams. Similar lamps were also carried by the electricians and mechanics, who were not to be feared, but if a 'shiny' was accompanied by the orange glow of a safety oil lamp it left no doubt whatever about who was coming because only gaffers carried these. So by keeping a careful look out for distant 'shinies' accompanied by 'safeties', one could always be sure of not being caught when the gaffers came around. I considered this to be the most important pit rule I ever learnt.

On the third day of the week Curly missed a shift, and I was told to take his place on the loader, leaving Levi to work on his own. At first it looked like an easy job. As each tub filled up it was pulled from under the loader and directed to me. I then had to give it a helping shove along about ten yards of track to a point where the tubs were coupled together into one large journey, ready for dispatch to the pit bottom.

In a way the job was reminiscent of the ones I had held on the Bank and in the pit bottom, though unlike the cage the conveyor belt from the face often stopped, sometimes for long periods, due to hold-ups on the face. Such respites always brought the Overman and District Fireman racing in, wanting to know what the hell was holding things up.

It was not long however before I realised that the full tubs needed more than just a helping shove to get them to the coupling point. I was having to strain myself to the limit to get them moving. Only by putting my back behind them and prising against the ground with my feet could I get them rolling turgidly along the track.

This naturally did not please the loader men who expected to have the full tubs cleared as quickly as possible so that when the next tub was filled up it could be pulled away and replaced with an empty tub shoved in from the opposite side of the loader. For most of the shift it was only by the skin of my teeth that I got rid of one full tub in time to make room for the next one. I streamed with perspiration, produced half by exertion and half by suspense, and kept puzzling why Curly had never complained about how strenuous the job was.

Meanwhile the loader men were cursing me for my laziness and calling me every name under the sun. Their jeers and abuse rang in my ears till tears of desperation mingled with the sweat running down my face. I was never so glad to see the end of the shift as I was that day.

The next morning Curly returned to the loader and soon discovered the cause of the trouble. On hearing that I was to work on the loader the men had deliberately raised the track, so that instead of pushing the full tubs downhill I had been pushing them up a slight incline. 'Now you see what I mean about watching out for yourself,' said Curly grimly.

On Saturday morning the Overman told Levi and me that he wanted us to go on the night shift, starting on Sunday. Though Levi consented, nights were the last thing I wanted: for one thing I did not see how I could go on the night shift and live in a hostel where I shared a dormitory with eleven other people.

'If you don't want it, tell him so,' said Curly, as ebullient as ever, when I hurried up to the loader to consult him at snapping. 'Come on Monday morning as usual. He won't send you back.'

So at the end of the shift I braced myself and told the Overman that I did not want nights. Unfortunately he would not take 'No' for an answer, but with Curly backing me up I told him I would not start night work on Sunday night under any circumstances.

On Monday morning I descended the pit and reported to the District Fireman as usual. He told me that as I was supposed to be on nights he could not book me in until I had seen the

Overman. The latter took one look at me and bellowed, 'I don't want you if you can't come when you're told! You can get back up the pit again for all I care!' He then stalked off, leaving me alone and bewildered in the pit bottom.

For a few moments I did not know what to do. Then I heard a voice over my shoulder whisper, 'Eh! Come 'ere you!' and saw the District Fireman beckoning me.

'Don't take no notice of him,' he muttered, 'He'll soon cool down. I want someone to drive the scraper motor in the top road and I reckon you'll do. It's a snip of a job, I can tell you, so you'd better get going before I change my mind! I'll put things right for you out here.'

The scraper chain was a conveyor on the face, electrically driven by a motor situated in the top road, about ten to twenty yards from the top of the face. The motor was contained in a heavy metal cabinet resembling a large old-fashioned office safe, with a small wheel, like a miniature driving wheel, on its front panel. To start the motor you turned the wheel slowly in a clockwise direction and to stop it you swung the wheel briskly the opposite way. All I had to do was start the motor when an adjacent bell rang twice and stop it when the bell rang once.

It was my first regular job down the pit and certainly my most comfortable. It wasn't long before I had made a seat at the side of the motor so that I did not have to get up to turn the wheel each time the bell rang; and I also adapted myself to respond automatically to the signals even though my thoughts might be far away, soaring above the ground.

Thus four weeks later when I went home for Christmas it was not such a gloomy picture of life that I painted round the family hearth, and with the end of the war in sight I felt confident that the new year would bring about my release from coal mining. It was fortunate that I could not see what was to come!

CHAPTER FIVE

The Top Road

WHEN I ARRIVED back at the hostel after the Christmas holiday I found the place in an uproar. A number of the lads, hurrying back to the station, met me at the gate saying, 'You might as well go back home!' but it wasn't until I reached my dormitory that I understood why. Huge icicles hung from the hot water pipes round the ceiling; my bed was covered with a sheet of frozen water, and in my locker everything was coated with ice. The whole block was like a huge refrigerator.

It appeared that the hot water pipes had been switched off when the hostel emptied for Christmas and had frozen up during the holiday, with the result that when the heating was switched back on they had all burst. This might not have been so disastrous if the pipes had occupied a normal position against the wall at floor level, but in every dormitory they were suspended from the ceiling.

As it was late at night the hostel housekeeper was fetching out all her reserve blankets and making up beds in the welfare block, the only place where the heat had been kept on during the holiday. When I entered the building it looked like an emergency hospital with beds on the floor of the study, lounge, cinema and games room. By the time I arrived most of the good beds had been taken and I finished up in an uncomfortable position under a billiard table, where I passed a sleepless night.

The following evening my dormitory mate, Jack, came to my rescue. He was on friendly terms with the hostel matron, she being partial to a drop of gin which he used to obtain for her, and she had allowed him and several others to occupy beds in the sick bay. When he told me there was still a bed vacant I wasted no time in claiming it for myself. With a radiator in each ward and spring mattresses on the beds a dozen of us slept in luxury for several nights, though at the end of the week one of the girls on the kitchen staff went down with an infectious complaint and we all had to turn out. By this time the dormitories had been reopened though the pipes were still out of order, the heating being provided by three feeble oil stoves down the centre of the room.

I continued to get up promptly at five thirty each morning, and when snow began to fall and buses failed to turn up I trudged part of the way to work without grumbling. By this time I had some travelling companions. The Pit Welfare Officer had noticed that I seemed to be travelling quite easily from the hostel and had ordered on the strength of this many more Bevin Boys than he could have found private billets for.

Most of the Bevin Boys at the hostel went home each weekend but a small number, including Jack and myself, were too far from home to do this and became full-time residents of the hostel, thus entering into our new life completely. We full-time residents, consisting of not more than twenty per cent of the hostel population, tended to stick together, particularly at weekends, and regarded ourselves as slightly superior to those who were in the hostel for only part of the week.

You were not considered to be a real inmate of Wimblebury Hostel until you had been out on a Saturday night expedition, which usually consisted of a long sojourn at the pub followed by dancing in the Community Centre. Your ticket for the dance consisted of a black mark stamped on the back of your hand when you paid the price of admission. Some of the boys tried to make their mark last from one Saturday night to the next but this proved impossible in such a dirty job as coal mining where frequent washing was unavoidable.

The two leading figures at the hostel were both unusual people. Simon was a lanky saintly-looking lad of eighteen who proposed to become a priest after leaving the mines. His chief object in life was to lead the hostel residents into the paths of righteousness, a full-time occupation for any one person. He organised weekly services in the cinema hall and spent a large amount of time canvassing among the residents to persuade them to attend. The response was always negligible but Simon never gave up trying and his services went on.

Blade – I never knew his first name – was a very different sort of person. A stocky, likeable figure with a shock of black hair, he was equally as fervent as Simon though his interest was politics, of which he took a vigorously left wing view. His alert eyes missed little that went on at the hostel, particularly on the management side, and one often wondered what ideas were simmering under that thatch of his. Stimulated by his knowledge and dining table eloquence some of the residents were already turning to him as a leader, though at this time Blade was content simply to hand round his political pamphlets. He was nevertheless a man to watch and take heed of.

The hostel was certainly a breeding ground for discontent. In such an isolated spot none of the amenities of the town was available and in the evening a cloud of boredom descended on the building, the interior of the welfare block being littered with sleeping figures sprawled over couches and armchairs. Entertainments such as whist drives and cinema shows were organised but these received little support and the residents seemed resigned to an apathetic life of working and sleeping.

Unfortunately in a number of cases the working side of life got pushed into the background. As we were paid according to the number of shifts we put in it was easy to take a shift off if we were prepared to lose part of our wages; and so on those cold mornings when the rain rattled on the tin roofs and the wind moaned outside, there were dozens who after being called by the nightwatchman turned over and said, 'To hell with the pit!' Absenteeism was highly contagious and in a hostel where so many lived together it spread rapidly. At this particular time it was frowned on in my dormitory which proved a model to the others, but alas even the sacred places were not immune and eventually we too succumbed to the disease.

There was however a certain Government official, the Regional Investigation Officer, whose job it was to stamp out absenteeism and anyone, either Bevin Boy or regular miner, who took more than four days off in eight weeks, was interviewed and either fined or in more serious cases taken before the Magistrates. Naturally where the Bevin Boys were concerned the Regional Investigation Officer had a busy job though at this period my worksheet was clean and I was able to evade his clutches.

From my seat beside the scraper motor in the top road of the South Shallow I was making considerable progress socially. As the motor was situated close to the top of the face, everyone going down the face used to get a minute with me before embarking on his journey. Having little to do apart from turning the wheel of the motor each time the bell rang I had ample time for conversation and in this way got to know most of the underground hierarchy.

The Manager or Under Manager came round once a week and the Overman once a shift. Their job – as far as I was concerned – seemed to be to find fault with everything. Twice a shift the District Fireman turned up, his job being to keep production going at full swing. Ever since he rescued me from banishment by the Overman I had been his devoted admirer and we became good pals. Also on my visitors' list were the mechanic and electrician permanently stationed in the South Shallow to supervise the apparatus. They often stayed at the motor for long periods in order to be on hand in the event of a breakdown on the face.

At the beginning and towards the end of each shift the tadger man and his mate appeared, the tadger being the heavy electric drill used in boring the shot holes in the coal face. The tadger man's routine was to start drilling at the top of the face, work his way down to the bottom and then return to the top for the end of the shift. His mate was with him to drag the thick cable which fed the electric current to the drill.

Following the tadger man were the Deputy Firemen who rammed the explosives into the shot holes and detonated the coal ready for it to be shovelled on to the scraper chain. The Deputies were responsible for everything concerned with the face and all breakdowns, bad conditions, etc., had to be rectified or reported by them. They were all miners who had obtained fireman's papers by taking a special examination at the local mining college.

The facemen came into the road several times during the shift when the Deputies were firing on the face. They were a different bunch from those using the middle road though much alike in appearance and to talk to. After the shift had been going an hour or two their bodies became plastered with dust and sweat though they always remained surprisingly cheerful. They swore like nothing I had ever heard before. We had been warned at the training centre that pit language was extremely colourful and this proved no understatement. The only word never tolerated was 'bastard' though I couldn't understand why because most of the others seemed worse if anything, but if this particular word was addressed to anyone it was automatically regarded as a deliberate provocation. All the other words were delivered in strings and reciprocated cheerfully, almost like liturgical versicles and responses.

At this time the facemen did not swear at me, not because of any regard for my feelings but because they wanted me to help them carry their pit props and other timber from the unloading point to the mouth of the face, a distance of roughly twenty to thirty yards. They also persuaded me to help them saw off some of the timber props to the length required, an ordeal that I used to avoid wherever possible. With me at one end of a two-handled saw and a faceman at the other it was a very uneven contest. Sometimes I used to feel that if they carried on sawing much longer my arm would drop off!

The timber consisted chiefly of six-foot props, known as 'trees', and flat wooden 'bars', drawn in from the pit bottom by a pony called Lion. Lion certainly did not live up to his name and was a bag of nerves. When you touched him a shiver ran through his body, and the slightest tap sent him careering down the road at a mad pace with his driver racing after him shouting, 'Come back, you bugger!' The pit ponies were well looked after in the underground stables but sometimes during the shift they suffered ill treatment at the hands of callous drivers.

The top road was the most interesting of the three roads leading to the South Shallow face. For part of the way it went through solid rock, a whitish sandstone which smelled pungently as you walked underneath it. This was said to be the safest part of the pit, the roof requiring no supports, though the road had to be baited frequently. Baiting was a widespread operation down the pit. Due to the enormous pressure pushing down on either side of the haulage roads there was a tendency for the floor to rise as well as for the roof to sink; so teams of men were employed to dig a layer off the floor of the roads in order to maintain a reasonable height between it and the roof and this was known as baiting.

There was also a steep gradient in the top road which had to be climbed on the way in each morning. At the summit was a well worn patch where everyone used to get a minute before proceeding further towards the face. Walking alone along the top road, either before or after the shift, I often marvelled at the great silence of the pit world. Such sounds as there were, such as timber supports creaking or distant earth rumblings, seemed to enhance the silence rather than diminish it, and the darkness was unlike anything encountered above ground. If you stepped into it without your lamp it swallowed you up like a black flood. One morning when I was walking in my lamp went out and I had to wait helplessly till someone came along whose lamp I could share.

The weather remained very cold during the early weeks of 1945 and it became almost a pleasure to quit the grey icebound landscape and descend to the warmth of the South Shallow. Though I was no longer working in the middle road Curly and I continued to be mates. If he got to the Bank first in the morning he collected my lamp and check for me and I did the same for him if I was first. This same loyalty did not apply at the end of the shift when it was up to every man to get back up to the surface as quickly as he could. If you got into the pit bottom soon after three o'clock you stood a good chance of getting an early ride to the surface, but if you left it later you had to tack on to the end of a long queue and wait a quarter of an hour or more for your turn.

There were many other Bevin Boys at the colliery, most of whom lived in adjacent towns and travelled home each day. I saw very little of them below ground because it appeared to be a policy of the Overmen not to have Bevin Boys working together but to attach them to groups of experienced miners. At some of the collieries on Cannock Chase Bevin Boys were directed into or could volunteer for the better paid heavy work but at Littleton we were all company men.

Pit workers were divided into two groups: contract men and company men. The facemen and skilled men on heavy work were employed by the colliery on a contract basis. Each contract group appointed its own leader known as a 'puffler', who collected the money or 'bag' as it was called, on Fridays and paid it out to the others in the pit canteen. Contract men could earn up to £20 a week, a large sum in those days, though they had to work extremely hard for it. Company men consisted mainly of haulage workers and were paid a fixed wage approved by the Mineworkers' Union.

As each week passed the distance to be walked in grew further. For six days a week the face pushed forward, gradually leaving behind my motor which had to be shifted forward about once a fortnight. One day it would be thirty yards from the face and the next only five yards, such adjustments being carried out during the afternoon or night shift. Sometimes when things went badly the facemen did not finish at three o'clock and I was required to work overtime on the motor. In order to keep my job I rarely refused though it meant walking at least halfway back to the hostel when I got to the top, the last bus having gone.

Actually the extra money I earned in this way was very acceptable because my week's wages were none too generous. For a full week of five and a half shifts I earned £3. 10s., from which I paid out approximately 10s. income tax, 2/6d. baths and insurance, 25/- hostel bill, plus 5/- for daily snaps and suppers, 3/- bus fares and 2/6d. laundry; so that after clothes and other essentials had been bought I did not have much to spare. And my financial situation grew worse when the colliery discovered I was in arrears with my income tax and deducted one pound weekly for five weeks.

This income tax business caused me several visits to the colliery offices where I joined a number of other dissatisfied workers waiting in a cold vestibule. After half an hour's wait I made my complaint to a nervous-looking office boy who then disappeared into the offices, returning later to tell me that the matter would be looked into. This boy acted as a sort of courier between the miners outside and the clerks inside, a crafty arrangement because no matter how dissatisfied the men were with their wages or income tax they had no opportunity of taking it up with those responsible, it being a waste of time to argue with the boy. We were treated with similar coolness at the Labour Exchange, where presumably the clerks derived their sense of superiority from the days of unemployment when they could influence a man's destiny almost with the stroke of a pen. I was glad that my future prospects did not depend on their goodwill.

During my term of employment in the top road I again ran foul of the Under Manager, who had not forgotten his first encounter with me on the Bank.

On one of his weekly tours of inspection he paused at the motor and said, 'Where's your safety lamp, boy?'

I replied that I didn't know I was supposed to have one.

'All motor drivers have to carry a safety lamp,' he said, adding that I should call at his office the next morning for an official permit.

After collecting both permit and lamp I arrived at the motor feeling very important and decided to test for gas. This was done by turning down the flame till it became a mere smudge on the wick and then holding up the lamp in the testing area. If a cone of flame hovered above the wick it meant that gas was present.

On this particular morning I held up the lamp to the roof and not only did a cone form above the wick but the lamp went 'pop' and blew out! When one of the Deputies came round I told him what had happened, but he just hissed 'Mind your own damn business!' and appeared to dismiss it at that. But shortly afterwards a bratticing sheet was hung across the road, this being a stiff canvas-like cloth, which restricted the flow of air causing a stronger current to blow the gas away.

The following week the Under Manager was grumbling at me again, this time because I hadn't got a driver's certificate. On his instructions I reported to his office the next morning, and was issued with a printed slip stating 'I hereby appoint you to attend to electrical switch gear and in the exercise of this authority you are enjoined to do so strictly in accordance with the Coal Mines Act and the General Regulations.'

On his next visit the Under Manager peered into the sand buckets kept by the motor for use in the event of fire and said, 'These buckets are half full of coal. Empty them out, pick out the bits of coal and put the clean sand back in the buckets again.' All this sounded a bit finicky to me but I did as he said.

The next time I thought he went too far. Rubbing his finger over the motor he said, 'This motor's covered with dust. I suppose you come from a clean home? Well, down the pit things should be kept equally clean and tidy.'

The idea of using a duster down the pit where fresh layers of dust settled every minute seemed ludicrous, and I might have treated his remarks as a joke had I not been stung by his reference to 'a clean home'. As it was I decided to embark on a silly puerile scheme of revenge.

Propped up against the motor was a battered old notice-board on which was printed a list of instructions for dealing with outbreaks of fire and cases of electric shock. During the following week I carefully memorised the contents of this board and the next time the Under Manager came along I substituted it for my usual seat and sat on it.

The trap was sprung and my victim walked straight into it.

'That noticeboard was intended for your information,' he said icily, 'It was not put there for you to sit on.'

'That's all right,' I replied confidently. 'I know what's on it.'

'Oh!' he exclaimed, smiling at the Overman and District Fireman who were with him. 'In that case perhaps you can enlighten the rest of us?'

'All right,' I said, and briskly recited everything written on the board.

For a few moments the Under Manager remained silent. Then, ignoring me altogether, he turned to the District Fireman, and said, 'This boy is bone idle. Shift him from here and give him some real work to do.' He then strode off in the direction of the face.

At once I regretted what I had done. In my impetuosity I had overlooked the one important hold that gaffers had on recalcitrant Bevin Boys which was to shift them off their current job to a less pleasant one. I had also forgotten Levi's golden rule about hanging on to a nice little job when you had one.

At the end of the shift I found Curly was in trouble too. The Under Manager had come across him 'sitting down with his eyes shut' and had ordered him on to nights on the spot. 'If you want to sleep during the day, then you can do it in your own time and not the colliery's,' was the Under Manager's succinct comment.

After the shift Curly and I sat drinking tea in the pit canteen consoling each other in our misfortune. It was Easter weekend but the day's events had cast a preliminary gloom on the holiday. After this I only saw him occasionally when he was coming out of the showers at the end of the night shift as I was hurriedly changing into my working clothes for the day shift. Though neither of us wished to admit it we both realised that afternoon in the pit canteen that our partnership was over.

CHAPTER SIX

The Tension End

THE SOUTH SHALLOW seam was six feet thick and rose at a sharp angle from the bottom road to the top. All the coal from the face was transported to the loader by the main conveyor belt, which emerged from the face into the middle road. This belt was fed on the actual coal face by two smaller conveyors, known as scraper chains, one running downwards from the top half of the face and the other running upwards from the bottom half. I of course was the driver of the motor operating the scraper chain on the top half.

Each scraper chain consisted of steep-sided metal trays dove-tailed together to form a continuous channel. Moving over the flat base of the trays was a ladder-shaped endless chain, the 'steps' of which scraped against the coal thrown on the trays and carried it along to the main conveyor belt. On reaching the main belt the chain rotated round a cog wheel and completed its circuit under the trays before re-emerging at the other end to commence its 'scraping' journey again.

When I returned to the pit from the Easter holiday I reported to the District Fireman as usual in the morning. 'The motor?' I asked hopefully. 'No,' he said, 'You've lost that job. I'm putting you on the tension end. Get along the bottom road. The facemen there'll tell you what to do.'

Walking along the bottom road I wondered what the tension end was and what sort of job I would be required to do there: the name itself sounded more like a psychological condition than a place of work.

On reaching the end of the road I introduced myself to the facemen sitting there eating sandwiches and told them I had been sent to work on the tension end. Having been employed in each of the three roads leading to the face I had now met in a fairly short time all the facemen working in the South Shallow district. They told me to get a minute: so I hung up my jacket on the side of the road and waited for the shift to start. From time to time I glanced towards the entrance to the face beyond which I had not ventured before though I suspected I might have to today.

After a few minutes I heard the scraper chain grinding into motion on the face, whereupon the facemen gave me a shovel and told me to follow them. They then led me out of the road, under a low horizontal girder and on to the face, which at that time of day consisted simply of the scraper chain gliding upwards on the side nearest the road, and piled up against it on the opposite side a great mass of detonated coal waiting to be shifted.

The bottom end of the chain was secured in position by two powerful wooden stays battened between the floor and the roof. These combated the efforts made by the chain when in motion to lift up or swing out of line: hence the name, tension end. The cog wheel at the end of the chain was enclosed in a flat metal box, open at one end. Through this aperture pushed a continuous flow of thick dust or slack, which due to the upward slope of the face kept sliding down the smooth trays to the bottom of the chain. If this outlet was not kept clear the cog wheel became choked, the chain could not rotate round it and the whole thing would go up in the air.

This then was my job: shovelling the slack as it seeped out at the tension end. No sooner had I thrown one shovelful on the chain than another would be forming at my feet, and so on ad infinitum. There was never a hope of the slack being carried away because it was too fine to be scraped along by the arms of the chain. Trying to keep the tension end clear was in fact as hopeless as carrying water in a colander or emptying the ocean with a sea shell. The more you shovelled the more quickly the slack gathered. And if you did not shovel the chain grew taut and began to writhe and rumble, despite the stays holding it down.

To begin with however the monotony of the job did not bother me because I was fascinated to be working alongside the miners on the actual coal face. As the only Bevin Boy or company man employed on the entire length of the South Shallow face I had a unique opportunity to observe all that went on there without being too involved in it myself.

At this period the South Shallow was the pride of Littleton Colliery. It was the most productive district in the pit and took precedence over all the others for men and supplies. The edict was that whatever else happened the South Shallow must be kept going. While they did not say much about it the facemen were obviously well satisfied with the workability of the seam and with the way in which the district was organised for drawing.

Work in the district went on all round the clock. During the afternoon or night shifts the main belt, scraper chains and other apparatus were moved a stage forward to keep up with the face. The coal cutter also traversed the length of the face, slicing the coal through a narrow vein of soft rock known as 'dirt', which ran through the seam like the filling in a sandwich. The cutter was a terrifying looking machine with sharp rotating blades which could easily cut to pieces anyone unfortunate enough to get in its path. After being cut the face was drilled and detonated ready for the facemen to start shifting the coal during the day shift.

The two hundred yard long face was divided into 'stents' of equal length, each faceman being responsible for removing the cubic area of coal in his particular stent and for erecting roof supports in it. Due to the slope of the face a certain amount of his coal inevitably rolled down to the next stent, involving him in a vigorous argument with his neighbour.

With the coal piled high to the roof, one of the first things the faceman had to do on starting work in the morning was to get down to the solid rock bottom of the seam where shovelling became more practicable. His main objective then was to get up a roof support: first a temporary foreset and then a mainset, both being wooden or steel trees supporting plank-like bars flattened against the roof. No man felt safe until he had got at least one foreset up nor satisfied till he had a mainset up, the roof being the least dependable feature of the face.

I feel sure I shall never see anyone work as hard as those men of the South Shallow. Once they had got a sweat on, as they put it, they stripped off their shirts and worked like this throughout the shift. The sweat streamed off their bodies, mingling with the dust till their skins seemed to have been painted with black enamel. Though they had much to try their patience they laboured indefatigably, losing neither their temper nor their vigour.

All day long the air was thick with dust. It got in your eyes, your mouth, your hair. It was particularly bad during the first half hour of the shift when everything was set in motion for the first time since the previous day. Then the dust, which had settled thickly overnight, rose up like a black fog, blotting out all but the nearest handlamps. The heat on the face was much greater too than in the haulage roads, and for the first time I had to start rationing my drinking water which I carried in a tin bottle slung over my shoulder. Several times I found I had emptied the bottle by snapping time and had to go thirsty for the latter half of the shift.

Standing at the tension end, with my back against the bottom wall of the face, I looked straight up the scraper chain, which rose gradually till it vanished into the murk of the upper face. On my right were the facemen working in their stents, and on my left the 'rippers', a team of three men who followed the face each day, extending the bottom road. There was a difference of several feet between the height of the face and the extra height required for the road, which meant that the rippers had to drop a fair quantity of the roof in order to put up their metal arched girders. Thus during the early hours of the shift they pulled out the trees supporting the roof at the mouth of the face, which crashed down with a roar, usually blocking our only exit from the face, especially if more roof came down than they had bargained for. The rippers then set to work clearing up the débris, erecting the arched girders and filling up the gaps between the arches with a patchwork of wooden slobs.

Also on my left, stretching continuously from the bottom road to the middle road, was the 'cog', the large empty area left by the removal of the coal during the previous shift. Using levers and chains the coggers pulled out the previous day's mainsets so that these could be used again by the facemen; they put up rough pillars of rock and old timber to discourage the roof from collapsing too hurriedly, and stacked off the area with dirt and rock though it was obviously impossible to fill it in as completely as it had been before. As the coggers withdrew the last mainsets you could hear the earth rumbling as it hastened to close up the gap which interfering man had made in it. I often thought that if a murderer wanted to dispose of a body he could not do better than put it in the cog where, once the supports had been removed, no one could ever find it or reach it again.

The tension end job was a dirty one and I used to be as black as the facemen when I entered the showers at the end of the shift. Getting my back clean was a major problem though someone usually barged under my shower, rubbing soap in his face flannel and saying, 'Give my back a rub, mate!'; and after I'd done his he would do mine. Often the intruder would not even bother to ask and I'd stagger under a vigorous back massage as a voice behind me said, 'That'll get it off, mate!' Of course I got my revenge when it was my turn to scrub him! Sometimes the old tattooed man from my section of the baths asked me to clean his back, offering me an unsavoury-looking rag to do it with. He never showed much appreciation of my efforts but I got a good deal of pleasure from watching the old masters on his back reappear from behind their coating of grime.

After a week or two on my new job I had added to my knowledge of pit lore, often by bitter experience. I learnt for example that if little particles of the roof dropped on the back of my neck it was a sure sign that something bigger was going to follow; and that if the wooden trees began to creak a weight was coming on and a temporary evacuation from the vicinity might be necessary.

I also learnt how to 'hog' my shovel. At the end of each shift the facemen started digging miniature graves or sliding back slobs on the walls of the road in order to hog, i.e. hide, their tools. This was a regrettable but necessary precaution because if the men on the afternoon or night shifts found your tools they would be sure to pinch them. Hence the more ingenious your method of hogging the more likely you were to retain your tools, and some of the hiding places devised by the facemen were very elaborate indeed.

Though I did not carry a watch I was able to tell the time by certain events recurring regularly each day. At eight o'clock for example the chain started up and at nine thirty the rippers dropped the ripping. At half past ten the tadger man and his mate reached the bottom of the face and drilled holes in the 'backs' — that part of the stent which could not be detonated during the night shift. At eleven thirty we had our snaps while the Deputy Firemen rammed the shotholes and fired the coal.

The man in the stent opposite the road put up a horizontal girder instead of mainsets and at one o'clock it was time for half a dozen of us to help him lift it into position. After two o'clock I usually helped the faceman nearest me to shift some of the coal from his stent. I hesitated to leave the tension end but did not like to refuse his aggressive demand for assistance, particularly if he was lagging behind the others. Anyway I soon got fagged out and had to return to my proper job, amazed at the stamina of the facemen.

For services rendered I was offered a chew of twist tobacco which the facemen carried in strings in their pockets, breaking off pieces as required. (When standing by a faceman it was advisable not to get on his spitting side, otherwise you were likely to be spattered with a mouthful of tobacco juice!) The first time I tried chewing tobacco I swallowed the juice and got enormous hiccups: so afterwards my services were given free of charge.

I soon got to know most of the men working at the bottom end of the face, and though I think they regarded me as a bit of a curiosity we got on well together. During snapping we all went into the road for our snaps and it was diverting to hear them talking. Their chief topics of conversation were either sport or sex, discussed in a ribald racy idiom which it would be impossible to imitate. Hearing them laughing and joking it was easy to forget how hard they worked and how close to them danger lurked in the shadows.

I had only been at the tension end two weeks when I first saw the coal stained with blood. Often when the face had been detonated certain tops clung stubbornly to the roof like fat lumpy stalactites. One morning some of these tops dropped without warning on a faceman working in his stent only a few yards from me.

The chain was stopped and the stretcher sent for by word of mouth, shouted from man to man up the face. The injured man was lying face downwards, unable to move but still conscious. It was suspected he had broken ribs though no one could say for sure. They carried him into the road and there he lay for half an hour till the stretcher took him away.

After this incident I always prayed that if anything happened to me it would put me right out so that I would not know the agony of that long wait or long journey to the Bank.

All this time great things were happening in Europe. On all sides the walls of the German citadel were tumbling before the Allied armies and the news of victory was expected hourly. The war which was responsible for my being in the mines but which I had almost forgotten in getting to grips with my new life was drawing to an end at last. We Bevin Boys of Cannock Chase impatiently awaited the news of Germany's surrender, partly because like everyone else in Britain we had been promised two days' holiday to celebrate the occasion, but mostly because we imagined that our release from coal mining would quickly follow.

On the evening of Monday May 7, I got tired of waiting by the radio and went off to the cinema in Cannock. When I came out flags were going up all over the place and people were celebrating in the streets with paper hats on their heads and brimming pint glasses in their hands. Realising that the news must have come through I hurried off towards the hostel, taking a short cut across the moor. On reaching the naked upland I saw coming towards me through the waving grass a stampede of Bevin Boys, armed with luggage and with jubilation written all over their faces. 'It's over! It's over!' they yelled at me as they went past. 'Coming home?' I did not see how they were going to get home at that time of the evening, particularly with all transport coming to a standstill: as for myself I was too far from home to try.

As the light faded everyone went up to the moor as if responding to an urge to get nearer the sky. Men, women and children dragged with them tree branches, old furniture, wooden boxes or any combustible object they could lay their hands on in order to build bonfires on the high ground. When it was dark the sky blazed with the glow of a dozen bonfires; voices laughing and singing came echoing across the moor; the night was full of rejoicing.

At midnight Jack and I stood on top of a derelict slag heap gazing at the vivid panorama around us. 'It won't be long now,' he said softly and I nodded my head in agreement. He didn't have to tell me what he meant. Demobilisation was always uppermost in our minds. If at that moment anyone had told me that nearly three more years of coal mining lay ahead of me I think I would have dropped dead on the spot!

The following evening a party of us from the hostel visited a workers' social club, the membership rules having been relaxed for the victory celebrations. Such clubs abounded on Cannock Chase, though the only advantage of being a member as far as I could see was that every three months or so when your membership number came up you were entitled to a certain amount of free beer.

It was one of the smaller clubs and everyone was cooped up tightly in a room where old-fashioned paper clung desperately to the walls. A hatch from which drinks were served occupied one corner of the room though it required a navigational feat to reach it, the floor space between it and the door being jammed with a multitude of people laughing, drinking and perspiring happily.

Seated in a row with their backs to the wall were several middle-aged matrons, clutching glasses of stout and presiding over the establishment like mute goddesses of woe. Though all was merriment about them they surveyed the scene with rigid funereal faces and watery red-rimmed eyes. A pale man was battering at the keys of a frightened piano as if determined to make more noise than all the rest of them put together while overhead a cumulus of cigarette smoke clouded the naked electric light bulb.

Our reception from the members was most hospitable. Orders were bellowed across the room and loaded glasses passed to us over the heads of the people, who frequently got wet in the process. Soon we were as light-hearted and light-headed as the rest of the company.

Balancing on a chair in the centre of the room was a young man, obviously tight, who was shouting, 'I'm going to die, ladies and gentlemen! I'm going to die!' At first nobody took any notice of him: then a middle-aged man with glasses, apparently known in the club, shouted, 'Quiet down, folks! Give the lad a chance! He really does die. I've seen him do it.'

On his recommendation everyone quietened down and an empty space was cleared in the middle of the room.

The young man then descended from his chair and explained what he was going to do. He claimed to be able to die temporarily by stopping his heart from beating, a feat he was now prepared to perform for our benefit. First however he required two persons with medical knowledge to examine him after his decease and verify his condition. The man with glasses and a Bevin Boy from the hostel both claimed to have been trained in First Aid and were appointed examiners.

A hush fell on the assembly as the doomed man took a deep breath, emitted an extraordinary sigh and collapsed flat on the floor as inert as a sack of potatoes. Everyone gazed expectantly as the two examiners did their work. Quite a stir was caused when the man with glasses, after completing his examination, looked solemnly round the room and declared portentously, 'This man is dead!' All eyes jerked quickly from him to the silent corpse lying crumpled on the floor.

Then it was the turn of the Bevin Boy to deliver his verdict on the deceased. 'It's all an act,' he said firmly. 'His heart and pulse may be a bit fainter than usual but otherwise they're beating normally.'

'You're a bloody liar!' yelled the man in glasses, jumping up and grabbing the Bevin Boy by the throat. 'That bloke's dead! You don't know nothing about First Aid!'

'Take your hands off me,' replied the Bevin Boy calmly, unperturbed by the angry murmurs coming from various parts of the room. 'I know as much about First Aid as you do! And I tell you he's not dead!'

'Don't take any notice of him! He's lying!' angrily retorted the man in glasses whose supporters were now closing in round our forthright comrade. After a quick consultation we others from the hostel formed ourselves into a spearhead to go to his rescue.

Meanwhile the manager behind the serving hatch saw that a storm was brewing, hurriedly closed down the hatch and came out front to preserve order.

Someone then struck a blow. Whether it was one of us or one of them was not clear, but the room was soon in an uproar amid which no one was more lively or vociferous than the middle-aged matrons who were now sparkling with animation as they exhorted their menfolk to combat. Though the mood of the others had switched from gaiety to anger, theirs had ascended from gloom to exuberation. 'Kick him up the arse!' yelled one of them to the man in glasses as he grappled with his co-examiner.

'Out! Out! All of you out! Especially the Bevin Boys!' cried the manager, trying desperately to clear the room without much success.

Fortunately, by sticking together, those of us from the hostel succeeded in rescuing our comrade and then retreated to the door: by this time everyone was arguing with his neighbour regardless of whether he was friend or foe.

The last thing I remember seeing as we squeezed out of the door into the street was the dead man returning to life, hammering his fists on the floor and shouting, 'I did die, I tell you! I did die!' but his protests were lost in the pandemonium about him.

CHAPTER SEVEN

The House of Commons

PARTY POLITICS HAD faded into the background during the war-time Coalition but after VE Day they returned to the forefront and I found myself involved in a spate of political argument both at the hostel and at the pit.

It began first of all in a humble way with the hostel residents' committee. This body was elected by the residents to organise social activities and to advise and negotiate with the hostel management, copies of the committee's minutes being regularly sent to the regional headquarters so that the residents' views might be properly aired.

Since its opening the hostel had been governed by a residents' committee consisting of an aloof group of Bevin Boys whose tenure of office resulted more from electoral apathy than from any mandate from the hostel population. Thus when the spring elections came along the radically-minded Blade and his supporters, who now had an almost universal following in the hostel, easily replaced this committee and took the government of the hostel into their own hands.

Blade's ambitions, however, extended far beyond improving the hostel menu, getting broken lights mended in the corridors or organising weekly tombola. His committee's aim was to unite the Bevin Boys in the country into a single militant body to press the Government for our early release from coal mining.

The formation of a Bevin Boys' organisation was badly needed but raised an awkward problem. Earlier in the year an enterprising Scoutmaster had founded a National Bevin Boys' Welfare Association – of which I became a member – but this had incurred the wrath of the powerful Miners' Union who didn't want minor organisations trespassing on what they considered to be their preserves. The Union's point of view was expressed in a letter sent by the general secretary and agent of the local branch to the residents of Wimblebury Hostel.

'Comrades,' it began, 'we address this appeal to you with the authority of the National Union of Mineworkers behind us: a union embracing 600,000 men – men who have fought battle after battle in the interests of all sections of the workers.

'The Bevin Boy who works in the pits alongside our miners is not a separate entity as unscrupulous individuals would infer. He suffers the same conditions below ground as the miner: an improvement in the miners' standard is an improvement of the Bevin Boys' standard. The Bevin Boys have been conscripted into the pits by State Law: the miners have been conscripted to the pits by Hunger, by an economic law, their only way to live under the present system.'

Referring to the National Bevin Boys' Welfare Association the letter went on, 'Assuming every Bevin Boy joined this association the total strength would only be 30,000. Secondly, before it could fight it would have to be recognised. Finally, the Bevin Boys would be isolated into a separate body, having no support from their class brothers, the miners, and thus would have their militancy and revolutionary aspirations crushed by the reactionary capitalist government and by tyrannical coal owners. The association will die an ignominious death leaving in its wake many deluded and demoralised Bevin Boys.'

The letter ended, 'Comrades, we are ready to fight your case but every Bevin Boy should join the Miners' Union, become active in its life so that we can go forward to fight for common interests of Bevin Boys and miners. Do not alienate yourselves from your allies, the miners, by falling into the trap of a separate Bevin Boys' association. The National Union of Mineworkers is your union! The miners' fight is your fight! Your fight is the miners' fight!'

But I could not convince myself that the miners' fight was the Bevin Boys' fight. I felt that we were indeed a separate entity and that our primary objective – release from coal mining – could never be shared by the miners. For this reason I decided against joining the Union even though the National Bevin Boys' Welfare Association soon fell by the wayside. Many of us also feared that joining the Union might be interpreted as an admission that we regarded ourselves as part of coal mining, when we knew perfectly well that our real jobs and interests lay in an entirely different sphere. Two years later when something akin to a closed shop was introduced in coal mining there was a long list of Bevin Boy abstainers at Littleton Colliery though this did not result in strikes as in some parts of the country.

Political controversy soon gripped the whole country. On May 20 the Labour members of the Cabinet resigned; the Labour Conference at Blackpool called for a General Election and polling was fixed to take place in July. Mr Churchill meanwhile formed what became known as the Caretaker Government and from then onwards the merits or otherwise of the Labour or Conservative Parties became the chief topic of discussion in the land. At eighteen I was too young to vote but this did not prevent me from taking an interest in what was happening.

There was not much doubt about which way the miners' votes were going. The bitterness they felt towards the Conservative Party cut terribly deep and sprang from the hardships they had endured between the two world wars when Tory governments were in power. They told me how work often came on only one or two shifts a week; sometimes they descended the pit and were already working when they were told to go back home without earning a penny. Many of them were obliged to take up a side line, such as coal hauling or a smallholding, in order to eke out a living. Nor had they forgotten the rigours of the General Strike or the person with whom they chiefly associated that event: Winston Churchill, whose part in subduing the strike had, rightly or wrongly, left him one of the men they most distrusted. And it was regarding Mr Churchill that the facemen's views and mine collided.

For several days I sat listening to them criticising him during snapping in the bottom road but kept quiet in order to steer clear of an argument. However I could not help feeling that whatever had happened in the past they had no right to discuss so unkindly the great leader who had brought us to victory. At length I could contain myself no longer and in no uncertain terms told them just how much I admired Mr Churchill and how much I despised them for their attitude towards him.

I don't know whether it was the eloquence of my oratory or the sudden discovery of a traitor in their midst that surprised them but the facemen sat in shocked silence for several moments before replying.

Then one of them cried, 'Why you're nothing but a bloody Tory!', as if this was an impossibility down a coal mine, and I was inundated with a flood of bitter rhetoric. Henceforth any reference to me was always preceded by 'that Tory so-and-so'; I was the victim of all kinds of horseplay, and at snapping twenty or more fire-eating radical facemen eagerly engaged me in heated dialectics. I knew nothing about party politics but everyone assumed from my defence of Mr Churchill that I was a Tory and I became stuck with the Party label.

Fortunately as the weeks went by it became increasingly obvious that the Tories were going to win the election, particularly in view of Mr Churchill's triumphant tours up and down the country: so I consoled myself that though I was in a minority of one at the pit, at least I was going to be on the winning side. Then on Thursday July 6, the country went to the polls and three weeks later, when the overseas Service vote had been counted, the election results were announced.

The first inkling I had of what had happened occurred at the end of the shift when after taking a shower I entered the crowded pit canteen. As I came through the door one of my adversaries leapt up and shouted for everyone to hear, 'Now what've you got to say about it, mate? They've kicked your gaffer, out!' This pronouncement was greeted with universal applause. At first I could not believe what he said but when press and radio confirmed the news of a Labour landslide I realised my position at the pit was likely to be uncomfortable for some time to come.

Soon after the General Election the first atom bomb was dropped on Hiroshima, precipitating the Japanese surrender and restoring peace to the world. VJ Day was also celebrated with bonfires on Cannock Chase though it was a considerably drier occasion than the previous victory day, most of the pubs and clubs having run out of beer. Once again there was a homeward stampede from the hostel, this second victory taking a toll among the residents, some of whom departed never to return.

With the arrival of September I completed my first year as a Bevin Boy. Up till then things had not worked out so badly; I had adapted myself to pit conditions and worked regularly despite the monotony of the work, but after this a deterioration took place. I got fed up with the job and the slow dry rot of boredom set in.

The first thing was that I no longer wanted to get up in the morning. During my first twelve months I had leapt out of bed at five a.m. but now I found myself whispering, 'Just five more minutes,' and instead of getting up I lay there calculating how I could wash in less time, dispense with cleaning my teeth, eat my breakfast more quickly, etc., in order to gain more time in bed.

My early morning timetable became so delicately adjusted that the slightest mishap resulted in my missing the bus.

But I soon discovered that rather than have this early morning rush it was far better not to get up at all, particularly when other fellows in the dormitory were doing the same thing and urging you to go with them on some enticing expedition during the day. Stolen fruits are said to taste sweeter and stolen days always seemed far more enjoyable than the Sundays we were entitled to have free. Fortunately one of the things the Labour Government did when it took office was to abolish the Regional Investigation Officer system, so there was nothing to stop us from taking shifts off apart from a reduced wage packet at the end of the week. For a great many boys this was not a sufficient deterrent and there was a stream of evictions from the hostel for non-payment of board though somehow I managed to keep my head above water.

Not wanting to get up in the morning, however, was only a symptom of a deeper-rooted malady. After six months at the tension end the monotony of the work was wearing me down. All through each shift I had to fight against a desire to drop off to sleep and after work my evenings were spent in a drowsy coma tucked up against a hostel radiator. I couldn't concentrate on any serious reading and on evenings out I usually offended the people I was visiting by dropping off while they talked to me. Even on short bus journeys I quickly fell asleep. Of course inhaling the stale air underground had something to do with it but it was more than just that. Being cooped up in a small space all day, shovelling an endless stream of slack, was having a completely demoralising effect. I grew to hate the scraper chain. I used to jeer at it, throw down my shovel and shout, 'All right! Pile up and break into pieces! I don't care!' but when it began rumbling or lifting up I soon relented and resumed shovelling. No matter how vigorously I protested the machine always won.

Matters were not improved by the men's attitude towards me. After the election I continued to be the butt of their humour and as my half-soaked condition developed I annoyed them more by making a mess of the simplest jobs. If I was asked to pass the axe I passed the hammer; if told to fetch a tree I brought a slob.

At times I thought of following the example of colleagues who had chucked it and gone home but I realised that sooner or later I would either have to come back in disgrace or go on the run. I felt a pang each morning as I passed the railway station on my way to the pit and saw the 6.30 a.m. train steam out bound for home, but though sorely tempted I managed to resist boarding it.

Meanwhile at the hostel the committee was going ahead with its campaign to unite the Bevin Boys. At mass meetings, which unlike Simon's services completely filled the cinema hall, delegates were appointed to tour other Bevin Boy hostels up and down the country to propagate the idea. Their railway fares came from donations ungrudgingly given by the hostel residents, now stimulated as they had rarely been before.

By this time however some form of action had become essential. Schemes of release for men in the armed forces had been announced but not a word had been said about what was to happen to the Bevin Boys. Some of us feared, unreasonably perhaps though it did not seem like it at the time, that we were stuck in the coal mines for good.

The delegates' tour was a great success. At hostels everywhere they were well received by Bevin Boys who were looking for just such a lead as was proposed, and it was arranged that a meeting of delegates from all over the country should be held in London in October. The committee had planned things on such a large scale that it was impossible to withhold enthusiasm and when our delegates left for London we awaited the outcome of the meeting eagerly. There were some who thought that these activities only made things worse for us while others optimistically thought that we would all be released within a month or two. All we could do now was wait and see.

For three days we heard nothing. There was no reference to the meeting in any of the daily papers that we turned to. Then at the end of three days our delegates returned with the welcome news that the London meeting had been successful and a Bevin Boys' organisation was to be formed.

Remarkable progress had already been made in campaigning for a Government statement on our release, for the day after the meeting the delegates had gone lobbying at the Houses of Parliament – with ironic results! Their reception from Labour M.Ps., we were told, had been distinctly frigid: in fact one who represented a mining area asked who had given them permission to leave work.

So they were apparently obliged to turn to Tory M.P.s. Here support was forthcoming and it was promised that the matter would be raised in the House.

But the delegates' most unexpected triumph was an interview with no less a person than the Minister of Fuel and Power, the redoubtable Mr Shinwell, under circumstances which I found hard to believe but which they described with aplomb. He had not made any definite statement but had promised to give consideration to our case.

On Tuesday October 23, Flight Lieutenant Teeling, the Conservative M.P. for Brighton, rose and put our case before the House of Commons in an eloquent, authoritative speech which earned him the gratitude of every Bevin Boy.

'I rise to bring before the House,' he said, 'the question of the demobilisation of what are commonly called Bevin Boys. In effect, that means conscripts for the mines and also a considerable number of optants. I am not trying to raise them in any political sense but merely for this reason: that I understand, and have understood for some time, that the Ministry of Labour have in mind making a definite statement about the position of these boys. Nothing, however, has been done yet and these boys remain where they are, not knowing what is to happen to them. They are not only constituents of mine but also constituents of almost every Member. There are well over 20,000 actual conscripts and nearly 30,000 optants, making a total not far short of 50,000 young men from the ages of 18 up to 22 and up to about 30 in the case of optants.

'These people, who have been brought from every part of the country have no mining background. They come from every class of the community and although they may be 100 per cent fit physically, many of them are entirely unsuitable for life in the mines. . . So far as I can see from a quick look at Hansard and what I heard myself, no reference whatever was made to these boys in yesterday's demobilisation debate. Yet in a sense they are mixed up with the Forces. When it was originally decided to try out this experiment the conscripts were boys who normally would have been called into the Services. Large numbers were in different Air and Army training corps when they were forced against their will into this calling.

'Certainly the country was then given the impression that these boys were, in a sense, doing the same thing as fellows called into the Forces. They complained that they would not have the glamour of being in the Services. Time and time again they were told and were given the impression that what they were doing was just as much a war-time job as any job in the Fighting Services . .'

Flight Lieutenant Teeling continued, 'Do not let us ever imagine that they intend to stay in the mines longer than necessary. I have been talking and travelling with them during the last month in Yorkshire, Northumberland, Cumberland and South Wales, and I can say, without exaggeration that I did not meet more than one per cent who had any intention whatever of going on with mining . . . What about their pay? These boys are not allowed lavish pay. They get about £3. 10os. a week, whereas the waiters in this House get almost double that sum. The same applies to hostels. I saw and stayed in one where there should have been 400 boys but where there were only 300. They were getting £3. 10s. a week. Certain deductions amount to about 7s.6d. and there is a further 30s. deducted for their hostel keep. That does not leave them with a very large income.

'Absenteeism is a growing trouble. I would like the House to picture these boys as having just left school with their careers and lives in front of them. Normally, up to a point, they would be kept by their families, or, if they were in the Services, everything would be done for them. They would be trained, educated and an eye would be kept on them; but these boys live in hostels, and although the staff do their level best, these boys are wasting their time completely when not down the mines. They have nothing to do and no one tries to find anything for them to do. It is true that they play billiards and ping-pong, and get reasonably good food, but the point is that now they have been told they will not be prosecuted for not going down the mines they are gradually drifting away.

'I met some of these boys who told me, "We only go down the mines now twice a week because that pays for our hostel keep." The rest of the time they waste hanging around doing nothing. Two other boys I met went down the mines very seldom and when it came to a night shift they did not go down at all. They were living in these hostels for young miners and they went off digging potatoes for local farmers. Another boy went off as a taxi-driver. They are compelled by law to work in the mines but when they get to the mines they are not compelled to go down them. They are hanging about and if you can imagine anything worse than that for boys of 18, 21 and 29, I personally cannot. These youths in large numbers have said to me, "We would rather be in the

Forces than here. It is wrecking our lives and we hate it like poison." They really do; you can see it in every hostel.

'This present absenteeism does not mean that you announce in the morning that you are going to be absent next day or next week; it merely means that you do not like the weather and you go back to bed again and do not tell anyone about it. The very fact that these boys do not turn up for work is completely upsetting the shifts and organisation of the pits for many hours, and means loss of a considerable amount of time. That is going to increase unless something can be done. I think it is up to the Government to do something fairly soon about it. I would beg of the Government if they do not feel they can make a statement on this matter today to realise that there are these reasons and that they are felt by thousands of boys all over the country. If these boys had been properly treated they might have become young ambassadors for the mining industry.'

After Flight Lieutenant Teeling's speech several Members spoke for or against him, but the crux of the debate came towards the end with the remarks of the Parliamentary Secretary to the Minister of Labour, Mr Ness Edwards.

'It is not challenged,' said Mr Edwards, 'that the principle of release applying to the Armed Forces should apply to the Bevin Boys. That is regarded, I take it, as being equitable and fair. In order that it should be clear and easily understood, what is in mind is that the date of demobilisation of the Bevin Boys shall be the date on which they would have been demobilised had they been in the Army. That, I imagine, is not only fair but is giving them almost favoured treatment.'

Flight Lieutenant Teeling: 'That is what they want to know.'

Mr Ness Edwards: 'The next point is in regard to the rights of reinstatement. Rights of reinstatement only apply to men in the Armed Forces, and to no one else. If it is to be given to the Bevin Boys, it must be given to the optants, to the volunteers and to every man who has been directed to employment in this country during the war.'

So that was that. There would be no reinstatement, gratuities or other privileges but at least we knew we should be demobbed sometime. Blade had therefore achieved what he set out to do: the Government had made the statement on release that we were all waiting to hear. But this statement came as a complete damper on enthusiasm. Now that it had been made there was nothing to fight for any more; the united Bevin Boys' movement disintegrated, having lost its unifying purpose; and all our dreams of an early release faded in this grey dawn of reality.

CHAPTER EIGHT

The Doldrums

THE APATHY I FELT towards my job was to a certain extent shared by the miners who after toiling for six shifts a week during the war years were now hoping to enjoy the fruits of victory and relax the pace a little.

This understandable reaction had a marked effect on the working of the South Shallow, for as 1945 ended fewer and fewer men turned up for work on Saturday mornings with the result that only one half of the face could be drawn off. This meant that a complete shift was lost each week for it was not possible to draw off the full length of the face on Monday when one half was in advance of the other, and with this loss of a shift on every district there was an appreciable decrease in output.

The machinery too began to show the ravages of wear and hardly a day passed by without the breaking down for anything up to an hour of some section of the district network. The scraper chain on which I worked started breaking down at least once a week causing a standstill of maybe half an hour during which it got so loaded up with coal by the facemen, itching to get on with their work, that it often had to be partly unloaded before the motor had strength to start it up again.

I hated the chain breaking. It always happened without warning, and if the outlet at the tension end happened to be blocked at the time I was blamed for the disaster. The breakage usually occurred as the chain went round the cog wheel at the tension end, one loose rung tangling up with the others, causing much grinding, snapping and contorting of metal. At the first sign of a breakage a signal was rung through to the motor driver who quickly brought the chain to a halt; the mechanic was then shouted for and he removed the broken length of chain, replacing it with a new length from supplies kept in the road.

Sometimes these breaks were really serious. During the first shift of the new year the chain had only been running for five minutes when it lifted up at the tension end, pulled free of the timber stays and swung up in the air. The man in the bottom stent pulled me clear while other men further up the face signalled the driver to stop the motor. By this time, however, the bottom end of the chain was ten or more yards up the face and the trays were buckled like a switchback railway. It was obvious that the job of putting it right would take all day and so the men on the bottom side were either sent to help their comrades on the top side or temporarily transferred to another district. Thus another shift was lost.

At least such breakages relieved the monotony. Other shifts went by uneventfully and I spent seven and a half listless hours shovelling at an interminable river of slack. With practice however I learnt to overcome boredom by entering into a semi-trance whereby my body automatically performed the function of shovelling leaving my imagination free to rove into more romantic spheres. I was amazed at how quickly the time could be made to pass in this way, though in a coal mine above all places it was a dangerous habit to cultivate and I had one experience that nearly put me in a trance for good.

The Deputy Fireman had some backs to fire in the bottom stent, and after ordering the men to a safe distance up the face he proceeded to make ready for firing the powder. To do this he connected his cable to the detonator wires in the shot hole, retreated up the face to where the men were standing, attached the other end of the cable to this battery and turned the key to fire. On this occasion however there was no explosion: so he went part of the way down the face to check his cable. As this did not appear to be faulty he again retired up the face and turned his key a second time. Once again there was no explosion: so this time he went right down to the bottom stent to check the actual shot hole. As he stooped to examine the hole he heard a noise behind him and was horrified to see me tucked away in the opposite corner, still shovelling blankly at the tension end only a few feet from the shot hole!

Grabbing hold of my arm he yelled, 'Get up the face, you bloody fool! Can't you see I'm firing?' Rudely awakened from my swim in the Mediterranean I hastily obeyed though without realising at first what had happened. It was not until I had joined the others further up the face that I learnt what a lucky escape I had had. 'I should think the Lord must be on your side!' said one of the facemen feelingly, and when at the third attempt the powder went off like thunder I was inclined to agree.

Another way in which I occupied my mind underground was in composing poetry. During the shift, while shovelling away, I thought up lines of verse which after much mental reshuffling were ready to set down complete on return to the hostel and pen and paper. Here is one of these poems composed underground: the subject,Cannock Chase.

Massive, bare –
An island rising from the lowland sea;
Of heaving moor with furry heather clad,
Coniferous woodland bristling sharp, erect;
Of unexpected valley, secret pool
And sudden pastoral scene.

Brooding, sad –
A casualty of man's despoiling hand;
Of brick-built rash and sordid avenue,
Misshapen pithead, grey, disconsolate;
Gaunt slag heaps looming through the mist and rain
And dismal sirens' moan.

Sullen, still –
The throbbing church bell sounds an empty note
And Sabbath mornings frugal comfort bring:
Uplifting thoughts of Heaven falter here
Where loveliness perverted lies above
And Hell so close below!

The others were equally morbid.

Early in the new year I changed my dormitory at the hostel. All the original members but one of my old dormitory had gone and their beds taken up by residents of newer vintage with whom I did not have the same bond.

The exception of course was Jack who was disgusted when I said I was moving out. The only time I ever heard him swear was at me as I closed the dormitory door behind me for the last time. However it turned out for the best because soon afterwards he was released from coal mining because of a deterioration in his health. I suspected this was partly due to his experiences in the ring. Though working regularly in the pit he still took part in evening bouts and often came home looking battered, though usually victorious.

Getting into a good dormitory was an essential tactic of hostel life. When the day's work started in the dark of the morning it was important that all the members of your dormitory should turn in at a reasonably early hour. One or more selfish people prowling about until midnight could easily keep the rest of the dormitory awake unnecessarily. Also it was desirable to be able to leave things about, such as towels on the hot water pipes or boots under the bed, without fear of having them pinched, and that your dormitory mates should have fairly clean ways. During my last weeks in my old dormitory a large pond of urine kept appearing in the middle of the floor during the night though despite various stratagems we were unable to detect the culprit.

My new dormitory had all the necessary virtues, its occupants being model residents. During recent months I had drifted away from my old drinking comrades, many of whom had vanished anyway, and had become friendly with a group who, though they relished a pint, were more often to be found in the hostel study than in the bar of the Miners' Arms. They were mostly students or apprentices, trying to keep up with their studies despite the demoralising apathy that pervaded Wimblebury Hostel in its lonely valley. They nearly all came from the same dormitory – B7 – and when a bed fell vacant there, approved me as its next occupant. One regrettable change from my old dormitory was that they were all regular workers and took a poor view of absenteeism. If I decided not to get up they tipped me out and made such a wreck of my bed that I had no alternative but to go to work!

Another departure from the hostel round about this time was the talented Blade whose residents' committee had gone into a decline since the Government's unequivocal statement on release the previous autumn. Attempts had been made by the committee to inspire fresh activity but the residents had retreated into their hard shells of complacency and were not to be tempted out of them again. The majority felt that as our rate of release had been linked to that of the army it was neither just nor practicable to conduct any further campaign; thus Blade's general meetings no longer attracted the multitude; even his committee seemed to lose interest in its affairs. After Blade left the hostel the residents' committee eventually returned to its old rôle as an unassuming consultant body between the hostel management and residents generally. Why Blade left or where he went to I did not know. He was only one of a number of residents moving on from the hostel at this time.

The first six months of the year were uneventful both at the hostel and at the pit, each succeeding week being much the same as its predecessor. On Sundays I used to do my chores such as washing my shirts and underwear or darning my socks, ironing coming on an evening later in the week. We had a regular washing circle in the ablutions on Sunday mornings when about a dozen of us gathered round the wash basins and talked over the affairs of the day while scrubbing our clothes clean. Once a month I used to tackle my pit clothes, though these were so black I was satisfied to get them a medium shade of grey, and the deep sediment of coal which accumulated at the bottom of the basin would have provided a useful supplement to anyone's coal ration.

I did not mind washing but darning was an anathema and after five minutes' stitching I drew both sides of the hole together impatiently and finished off the job in this clumsy fashion. Most of the darning for my pit clothes was done underground with lengths of shot wire. After the coal had been fired it was easy to find this thin silver wire which was useful for holding together the seat of your trousers or the arm of your coat.

I was reunited with an old friend when Lion the pit pony was transferred to the bottom road to draw in timber and other supplies, though he played a mean trick on me one morning. Most of the men carried their sandwiches in special snap tins to keep out the mice, or 'moggies' as they were called, which infested all parts of the pit. These little creatures, not much bigger than your thumbnail, used to run up and down your legs or arms during snapping, hoping to catch any crumbs you let fall. I felt sorry for them living out their existence in the dark underground world where food could not have been plentiful. Unlike the other men I carried my snap wrapped in a newspaper and though the moggies had occasionally got at it they had never consumed more than one sandwich. On this particular morning however I found that the whole lot had gone, newspaper wrapping and all. I was saddened when told that Lion had been seen nosing in my jacket pocket and was undoubtedly the culprit.

'I'm turning my back,' said the pony driver, moved by the gravity of Lion's offence. 'Punish him as you think fit.'

I agreed that Lion should be taught a lesson and advanced towards him with a wooden locker in my hand and a 'this is going to hurt me more than it does you' look on my face. Unaware that he was still hooked on to a journey of tubs that he had just brought in from the pit bottom I gave Lion a wallop across his hind quarters, causing him to turn and run off in the opposite direction: alas! pulling off three loaded tubs in his flight. By this time the pony driver's back was no longer turned and when he saw the three upturned tubs it was his turn to seize a locker to use on me! Like Lion, I also ran!

At the beginning of March we were told that we could apply to the Labour Exchange for our release group number, mine being 63. At that time they were only just demobbing Group 30: so I could see that a long stretch of coal mining still lay ahead.

One of the residents of Wimblebury Hostel however received his release from coal mining tragically sooner than expected. He was an ordinary lad, just one of the crowd: the sort of inconspicuous person one remembers vaguely but cannot easily pin a name to. While working in a haulage road underground he was caught in a moving journey of tubs, dragged along the track and crushed to death. Many hundreds of young men the same age as himself had died serving their country as soldiers on the battlefield. It was his destiny to die serving as a miner underground.

Simon arranged that his weekly service in the cinema hall should take the form of a memorial service and invited the local parish priest to officiate. Considering the poor attendance at all previous hostel services this was a bold step but it proved justified. The hall was filled to the doors, many residents having to stand in the vestibule outside. There were only a dozen hymn books among ten times that number but the hymns were the old ones that everyone knew and were sung with great feeling. It was a moving experience for us all, but particularly for Simon who after all this time had seen the hall filled for one of his services. He must have regretted that it had to be under such tragic circumstances; however the hall was never quite so empty for his services again.

During the summer the Ministry of Labour carried out a purge among Bevin Boys and all those tactfully described as misfits – actually habitual absentees – were transferred into the army. The task of sifting the bad from the good was carried out by our old friend the Regional Investigation Officer, who also had the job of tracing the Bevin Boys long since disappeared. Most of the misfits were glad to get into the army, this having been their objective all along; but one point which was not satisfactorily explained was how the transfer was going to affect demob. We were led to believe that the time already spent in the pits, now well over two years, would not count and that those transferred into the army would be starting from scratch. And glad though many Bevin Boys were to go into the army they had no desire to let themselves in for an extra two or three years before being able to return to civilian life again.

This was an unpleasant time for us all. Rumours flashed across the area about Bevin Boys who had been sent their army papers despite the fact that they had been working regularly, the only thing against them being that they were disliked by a particular Overman or other pit official. With the shadow of victimisation hanging over us it became urgent to take some form of protective action though the obvious person to provide a lead – Blade – had gone, nor were the residents of the hostel in any mood to meet or even discuss the situation. They had had enough of controversy. So it was at Littleton Colliery, the local pit employing the largest number of Bevin Boys, that the first move was made.

The majority of Bevin Boys employed at Littleton travelled to and from their homes each day, the colliery being closely situated to a main bus route connecting with several large towns not too far away. These Bevin Boys had little or no association with each other. During the shift they were split up among the various districts and various groups of miners and afterwards were in too much of a hurry to catch buses home to have any real contact with others of their kind. Living at home they had missed the tide of militancy inspired by the united Bevin Boys' movement the previous summer: indeed the only time they had been with other Bevin Boys en masse was during their month at the training centre.

Thus when a meeting of Bevin Boys from Littleton Colliery was called in the Co-op. Hall at Cannock it was a novel experience for most of them and they flocked to it in large numbers despite the fact that many of them had anything up to twenty miles to travel home in the evening. After a chairman had been elected all the old ideas, which those of us from the hostel seemed to have been hearing for years, were debated – the need for Bevin Boys to organise, etc. – but for most of the audience such ideas were falling on fresh willing ears and the response was enthusiastic.

The outcome of the meeting was reported as follows in the *Wolverhampton Express & Star.* 'In order to direct public attention to various grievances and to press for a ruling that time spent in the pits would count towards service in the Forces by those transferred, a meeting of Bevin Boys employed at Littleton Colliery decided at Cannock last night to form a committee representing all Cannock Chase Bevin Boys . . .

'Referring to the announcement that Bevin Boys who were misfits in the mines would be drafted into the Forces, the chairman said they wanted to know if the question of those who were misfits was to be decided by the managements or by some representative bodies. If the managements alone were to decide, he feared victimisation. He had heard of cases where Bevin Boys working four to five shifts a week had received papers for the Army.'

Following this meeting a printed questionnaire was distributed among Bevin Boys at Littleton Colliery who were asked to answer the questions with an appropriate 'Yes' or 'No' and return the form to the committee. Two of the questions were:

Are you willing to become organised? (Yes)

Do you agree to the 56 days threat? (No) This, it was generally felt, was a very unfair condition of release which stipulated that if any Bevin Boy had not found employment within 56 days after his release he would be redirected back into the pits again. As far as I know this condition was never rescinded.

I took a number of the questionnaires to the hostel where I persuaded some of the residents to fill in their replies, many of which proved to be flippant. However, after this the Cannock Bevin Boys' committee didn't know quite what to do next, their new-found ardour petered out, and I was left with a batch of signed questionnaires on my hands.

The dismal summer far from petering out ended with a deluge, adding a great flood to the annals of Wimblebury Hostel. Working underground it was obviously impossible to know what sort of weather was happening up above. The only clue came from the condition of the tubs, which made several journeys up and down the shaft during each shift. Ice on the tubs spoke of frost, dampness of rain, and dryness – even warmth to the touch – of fine weather. Another way in which tubs were helpful to underground workers was in conveying the latest news sensations or sports results, chalked on the side of descending tubs by obliging banksmen.

During the summer of 1946 many more damp tubs came below than dry ones and on most days we ascended from the dry warmth to be greeted with grey skies and drizzle on the Bank. Things culminated in a day of torrential rain on which it was my misfortune to miss the bus back to the hostel with the result that I had to walk, taking a short cut across the open rain-washed moor. I arrived at the hostel shivering, soaked to the skin and looking forward to a warm bath followed by a change into dry clothes.

From outside the hostel looked the same as usual but on approaching my dormitory block I was startled to see water gushing out of the entrance doors, and on going inside I was confronted by a boisterous torrent pouring down the corridor, swirling in and out of the dormitories and cascading down the steps. The only person in sight was the hostel housekeeper who though long past the age for that sort of thing had tucked the ends of her overall in the lower reaches of her underwear and was paddling in and out of dormitories on salvage work.

'What's happened?' I gasped at her.

'Oh, it's all this rain we've had,' she replied. 'The hills can't take it any more. This block must have been built on the dry course of a stream. The water's coming straight in at one end and out the other.'

She added that the occupants of the block had sought dry refuge elsewhere and advised me to do the same; then gazing affectionately at the torrent below she went on, 'You know, the water really is beautifully clear and it's not a bit cold.' By this time my teeth were chattering and with a grumbled 'I'd sooner do my paddling by the seaside any day,' I waded into my dormitory.

As usual when I opened my locker door a whole number of articles tumbled out though this time they hit the floor with a splash instead of a thud and started to float away. The contortions I performed in changing my clothes while standing on top of the bed would have done credit to a music hall act but eventually I was ready to paddle off, unshaven and unwashed, with my trousers rolled above my knees and my shoes and socks hanging round my neck, to the dining hall for my tea. Fortunately the welfare block had escaped the worst of the disaster.

The flood subsided sooner than had been expected and by mid evening had run itself dry, leaving a few isolated pools and a large amount of sediment behind: so we all moved back into our dormitories again, the loathsome oil stoves being re-introduced to dry out the damp. Unfortunately the invading stream, having established this precedent, did not hesitate to take the same short cut through the dormitories on several future occasions and one night we all went to bed with water still swirling merrily underneath us.

CHAPTER NINE

The Roll

THE AUTUMN OF 1946 saw the coming of the roll and the beginning of the end of the prosperous South Shallow district: conditions on the face slowly worsened till they became a nightmare. When it first appeared about halfway up the bottom side of the face the roll was slight and affected only a few feet in a particular stent: it was a contortion or fault in the coal seam, the roof and floor going up and down abruptly like a camel's hump; but it then started to move slowly down the face, getting more marked from day to day, till the faceman in whose stent it was had to erect an eight foot tree in one half of the stent and a four foot tree in the other.

Soon the men on the afternoon shift were unable to get the coal cutter under the low part of the roll, so the faceman concerned had to hack at the roof with his pick in order to level it off to a reasonable height. However tampering with the strata above a seam is a risky business, particularly in the vicinity of a fault. Thus when the faceman probed the roof with his pick he usually brought down far more than he wanted, with the result that on most afternoons the men on the bottom side of the face had to rally round their unfortunate comrade who at the end of the shift had more stuff – mainly rock – to shift than he had had to begin with.

After a fall the débris had to be partly cleared before roof supports could be erected which meant that the facemen had to work under a roof of naked sandstone. This was a real test of nerve because unlike the coal this rock gave no warning of an impending fall and spinning knife-sharp fragments caused nasty wounds, not to mention the murderous larger pieces. However the facemen were not the sort to be scared of this sort of thing and continued to draw off the face as usual. The job was more difficult but still had to be done.

Nevertheless it was with growing anxiety that the downward movement of the roll was observed. In a week or two's time it was going to meet with the junction of the bottom road, and once the rippers started dropping part of the roof to extend the bottom road it was possible they might collapse the entire bottom end. The Manager, Under Manager and Overman, all wearing solemn faces, paid regular visits to inspect the development of the roll and discuss what effect it was likely to have on the face, but there was only one thing they or anyone else could do and that was to wait and see.

During the autumn the Cannock Chase Bevin Boys' committee was roused from slumber by the Government's latest statement on release, which angered both members of the Forces and Bevin Boys. We were told that although Group 46 on the army scale would be out by Christmas, only three more groups would be released during the following six months, i.e. up to June 30 1947. We read newspaper reports of unrest in the army in the Middle East and felt that if soldiers had courage to protest we, who were not subject to military discipline, certainly ought to back them up: so on Friday November 15, the committee called a meeting extraordinary in Cannock town.

About one hundred Bevin Boys attended, most of them employees of Littleton Colliery interrupting their evening bus journey home. Though the attendance was good it was nowhere near representative of Cannock Chase Bevin Boys as a whole. I felt sure, for instance, that the majority of hostel residents would dissociate themselves from any campaign, but the Bevin Boys present were the day travellers who, apart from the summer meeting, had not had any previous opportunity of getting together after hours; they thrilled at finding themselves part of a crowd after functioning as individuals for so long and lapped up all the old bold ideas, such as uniting the Bevin Boys, sending delegates to other mining areas to rally support for the cause and, above all, making an emphatic protest to the Government against the slowness of demob.

Those of us from the hostel told the meeting of Blade and his efforts to achieve what they suggested, but it was no use. The boys wanted action and were determined to get it. What sort of action, they had been whispering about in groups at the pithead for several days. I leave it to the *Wolverhampton Express & Star* report of the meeting to tell its melancholy story.

'Cannock Chase Bevin Boys have decided on a two-day protest strike because of their slow rate of release from the mines. At a meeting held in Cannock yesterday afternoon, Bevin Boys from pits in the Chase district decided by ballot to hold the strike on Monday week to show their disapproval of the Government plans to release boys from the pits more slowly than originally planned.'

The days leading up to the strike were the most hectic I experienced as a Bevin Boy. As I expected, most of the hostel residents refused to support the strike: in fact they ridiculed the idea. They were prepared to write to their M.Ps. complaining about the slow demob. but considered this was enough. Thus each day I found myself alternating between hot and cold. At the pit the Bevin Boys were in a fever of excitement, taking it for granted that the world was on their side, while at the hostel the atmosphere froze at the mention of the word strike and the conversation was quickly changed to another subject.

The major event of the pre-strike period was a visit to the hostel of a Ministry of Labour inspector. One might have expected some fiery-eyed titan to have been sent down to quell the trouble but he turned out to be a polite middle-aged man whose friendly discourse ambled through a forest of clichés.

'Don't rush blindly into this strike, lads,' he said to a small gathering of Littleton employees in the hostel study. 'You won't change the laws of the Medes and Persians that way. What you propose to do is entirely unofficial: you have no union or other backing for it. Moreover you are required by law to give three weeks' notice of a strike but you have given none. Look before you leap, lads! I know you may have grievances but this is not the way to ventilate them. If you go on strike you'll simply be jumping out of the frying pan into the fire!'

Though the man himself was gentle enough I was alarmed that the Ministry should have thought his intervention necessary and the first day of the stoppage did not approach without trepidation on my part. The miners were completely cynical about the whole thing. 'It won't do you any good,' said the older ones. 'Strikes never do.' Some of the more unkind ones added, 'The output will probably go up anyway.'

On Monday November 25 1946, the first day of the 'mass' strike of Bevin Boys on Cannock Chase, I lay in bed at 6.30 a.m. and watched the eleven other Bevin Boys in my dormitory troop off to work. It was a bad start. But when I went down to breakfast I was heartened to see at least all the other Littleton boys living at the hostel had stayed out. The reports in the evening papers were not so heartening however. This was one:

'Bevin Boys on Cannock Chase started a two day token strike today against the recent Government announcement of a reduced demobilization rate . . .

'An official of the Cannock Chase collieries said that there was no indication of a 100 per cent strike among Bevin Boys employed there. "We have Bevin Boys at work this morning," he said. "There are a certain number of absentees but we always get that on Monday mornings. At present there is no means of telling whether the absentees are strikers or otherwise. It is not affecting our work in the slightest."

'A representative of the Cannock Chase Miners' Association said that if action had been taken by the Bevin Boys it was unofficial and no representations had been made to him. In his opinion the whole thing was "rather a damp squib".'

This reference to a damp squib made me wince: it was much too near the truth, but perhaps it was because the strike was such an utterly damp squib that we escaped without reprimand. Once the two days were up we all returned to work and were allowed to carry on as usual. Other pits had discovered no remarkable decrease in attendance but at Littleton we had stayed out to a man: in fact it might just as well have been a Littleton strike. We all expected reprisals but there were none; it was rumoured that we should be directed into the toughest section of the army under the supervision of Britain's most sadistic sergeant majors but this never happened, and as for demob. this remained as slow as ever.

Yet the strike was successful in clearing up once and for all the recalcitrant spirit that had pervaded the Bevin Boys for so long. As a result of the summer purge most of the malcontents had been removed into khaki and those who were left developed into regular conscientious workers, no longer thinking primarily in terms of demob. the sooner the better, but accepting the life that had been thrust upon them and trying to make a success of it. I think this was true not only of Cannock Chase but of all other mining areas; indeed, as far as the world at large was concerned, I doubt whether the Bevin Boy was ever heard of again, though his most useful period of service was just beginning.

Below ground disaster was threatening the bottom end of the South Shallow face. By mid-November the roll had reached the junction of the bottom road with the face – with grim consequences. Each day as the rippers dropped the portion of roof overhanging from the previous day's shift in order to erect the 12 foot arches of the road, down tumbled a mass of rock, including part of the roof of that current day's working. This left a lofty dome in the roof which the rippers had to fill in with timber after erecting a supporting framework of arches. Normally the facemen working in the bottom end carried on with their work while ripping was in progress but because of the doubtful reaction of the roof they now had to retire temporarily into the bottom road, I of course accompanying them.

When the rippers drew out the last supports there was a tremendous cracking noise as the roof collapsed, sending up a thick cloud of dust which billowed along the road towards us like a grey genie released from a magic bottle. The rippers then took long slobs and prodded at the ceiling in order to bring down any loose pieces: when it was safe they beckoned us to crawl back under to the face. Several times however there were such heavy falls that the rippers had to shovel away some of the débris before there was a hole big enough for us to squeeze through. Of course the men working in stents further up the face above the roll were unaffected, and when I returned to the tension end a mass of slack had accumulated for me to shift.

By this time the roll had become a huge size, curving up and down in a fantastic loop and affecting not only the stent in which it was located but several others on either side. Extracting the coal from the seam in the affected area became increasingly difficult owing to the faulty nature of the strata, which weakened both the roof and floor of the seam. At length it became obvious that it was neither safe nor practicable to continue with the bottom side as it was; the gaffers held consultations and a drastic manoeuvre was adopted to bypass the roll. It was decided that the bottom road should turn sharply left and go up to join the middle road, and that the bottom side of the face should be amputated, only the top twenty yards well above the roll to remain. Thus the South Shallow district which had long been the glory of No. 3 Pit was reduced to crippledom by the roll.

The transition was completed within a few shifts, the face now having only two approach roads – the top and the middle roads. The bottom side of the face consisted merely of a short extension or cul-de-sac, about 25 yards long, in which five men had their stents. A chain still operated on this side but it was so short that a man at the tension end seemed hardly necessary. However for some reason best known to themselves – perhaps because they foresaw what was going to happen – the gaffers retained me on my old job and I had my leg pulled a great deal about idling away each shift, lying on my back. Having no excuse to do otherwise I used to help Jim, the man in the bottom stent, to shift his coal, finding the task easier than I had done when I first arrived at the tension end. As he knew I didn't chew he occasionally rewarded me with an apple produced from his snap tin.

Because the bottom side was a dead end there was no air current circulating in it, consequently it was very hot. For the first time since becoming a Bevin Boy I was obliged to work with my shirt off, the colour of my skin soon turning the colour of the coal seam, camouflaging me like a chameleon. The air current travelling from the middle road up the face was supposed to be drawn down the bottom side but the ventilation was not at all good, especially in the bottom end, where unpleasant smells loitered round a long time.

All went well for a week or two: then there was every indication that the roll, which had been left safely below, was now moving upwards. As its outer tentacles penetrated the bottom wall of the face, the roof and floor began writhing in a now all too familiar manner; there were more inspections by the gaffers and rumours went around that the roll would eventually travel from one end of the face to the other, but the facemen's orders were to carry on.

With the upward advance of the roll the floor of the seam became steeper and the chain tilted at a sharper angle so that far more slack began sliding back to the tension end. Soon it was pouring out in greater quantity than it had ever done when the chain was four times its present length, making it impossible for me to keep up with the flow. As the chain was so choked up with slack it was taking a certain amount up with it, so the Deputy Fireman put another Bevin Boy, called Cuckoo, at the top of the chain where it emptied into the main belt in the middle road, with instructions to ease the flow at my end by keeping the top end clear. How often afterwards did I bawl at that wretched youth who when pausing in his shovelling left me overwhelmed at the other end!

Soon the roof at the tension end was barely three feet high and I had to work all day on my hands and knees. Up till then I had usually been the last person to enter the face in the morning but now I had to be the first because the tension end was so choked up that the chain could not move till the bottom outlet had been cleared. As there was only about a foot between the top of the slack and the roof it was not much use trying to shovel: so the Deputy Fireman got hold of my legs and lowered me head first down the chain, thus enabling me to scrape the end clear with my hands.

With so little space in which to move and so little air to breathe working conditions on the bottom side became deplorable, but the gallant facemen drew off their stents every day, their knuckles, elbows and backs becoming red and raw with the scratches they received in trying to shovel under the low roof.

For me the nightmare came each time the chain started up. By this time the trays were at such a steep angle that the chain could only scrape away small lumps of coal: the bigger lumps came bounding down over the rungs to me at the tension end. I shouted myself hoarse urging the men not to throw big lumps on the chain but they were always forgetting and I became a perfect sitting duck. Crouched in a space only three feet high with a thick stay on either side of me I watched helplessly as the lumps came bouncing down, unable to move myself in any direction. Often they bumped off the chain into the bottom stent, producing a loud explosion from Jim, who seemed more offended at having someone else's coal to shift than at nearly being knocked out by it.

The end came in December only a few days before Christmas Eve. Fortunately it happened after three o'clock when the men had finished work and the face was deserted. I knew nothing of what had happened till I reported for work the next morning. I was told that a severe weight had come on during the afternoon shift and that the bottom side was no more. This meant that the South Shallow face now had only one side left, the 120 yards stretching from the middle road to the top road, and that for the first time for eighteen months – a record run in one job for a Bevin Boy in No. 3 Pit – I was out of a job.

CHAPTER TEN

The Cable Dragger

THE NEW YEAR began with the nationalisation of the coal mining industry by the Labour Government. 'Today, January 1st, 1947, will be remembered as one of the great days in the industrial history of our country. The coal mines now belong to the nation. This act offers great possibilities of social advance for the workers and indeed for the whole nation. If all alike – workers, National Coal Board and Government – shoulder their duties resolutely and use their rights wisely, these great advances will be assured. I send my best wishes to all engaged in this vital work.' Thus ran the message from the Prime Minister, Mr Attlee, as the mines passed from private ownership into the hands of the people. We were no longer working for Littleton Collieries Ltd. but for the National Coal Board, Littleton Unit.

On Sunday January 5, brass bands led processions of pitmen to the various collieries for the hoisting of blue National Coal Board flags and the erection of notices, proclaiming: 'This colliery is now managed by the National Coal Board on behalf of the people.' Promptly at half past eleven the pit hooters wailed out in unison across the hushed valleys of Cannock Chase and in the still of the Sabbath morning a new era in coal mining began.

But work on Monday morning was no different from usual. The gaffers, the day's routine, the underground life were all unaltered; though the colliery had changed ownership it still functioned the same way as before. In this respect the introduction of nationalisation was lacking in showmanship. One looked in vain for some vivid innovation which would stamp forever in the miners' minds a first firm picture of advancement that no later misunderstandings could remove. As it was, January 1947 might have been January 1945 or 1946. There was no noticeable difference.

Despite this defect the men of Littleton Colliery were optimistic and did their best to make a success of the new enterprise. There were jocular remarks, such as 'I'm a civil servant now!' and 'Mind what you're doing to my mine!'

Unfortunately No. 3 Pit got away to a bad start with its major productive face, the South Shallow, crippled by the roll. However the top side continued to draw normally though it was anticipated that the roll, which had destroyed the bottom side, would undoubtedly move upwards in the course of time.

When I returned from the Christmas holiday I was given a new job as tadgerman's mate. The tadger, the drill used for boring shot holes, was connected by a long rubber cable to the power in the middle road and it was my duty to see that wherever the tadgerman was on the face he always had enough cable to operate comfortably.

My new job was unlike anything I had ever done before: it was a farce, an outrage, a fiasco, an ordeal, a humiliation, a nightmare, a masterpiece of disorder.

The reason for this was that wherever the tadger man and I moved on the face we were trespassing in a stent where a faceman was working. Though an individual faceman might crave our services for drilling a shot hole in obdurate coal, all the others whom we encountered in reaching him regarded us as confounded interlopers. In fact each shift developed into a running battle between the facemen and the tadger man and his mate, particularly the latter, who being responsible for the cable tended to get in the way more than his senior partner.

For example, as we traversed the face first thing in the morning the coal was piled up to the roof with each faceman striving to excavate a patch of hard bottom on which to erect a protective foreset. My attempts to haul the cable through a particular stent usually set the coal rolling in a miniature avalanche, thus burying the patch which had been excavated, whereupon the faceman concerned threw down his shovel in a rage, begged Heaven for patience, and scorched me with invective of a most personal wounding kind. Also, wherever I coiled up the cable always seemed to be the wrong place for the faceman in whose stent I was located. If I refused to move it he picked up as much of the cable as he could lift and either threw it at or over me till I collapsed looking like a kitten tangled up in a ball of wool.

I became the most abused maltreated person on the face— and liked it, the job being a merciful deliverance from the monotony of the tension end. Instead of being cooped up in one place doing the same thing all day I was now on the move, going from stent to stent and meeting all the facemen. Though quick-tempered and voluble the facemen cooled off quickly and bore no grudge: as I got to know them better I liked them better; if they bawled at me I bawled back at them, and we got along tolerably well that way.

Though I continued to be a company man, paid the fixed rate of £3. 10s. per week, the tadger man, being a skilled heavy worker, was on contract, being paid out of the facemen's weekly bag. He collected his wage from the puffler in the pit canteen each Friday. In view of the hazards that he and his mate had to undergo it was important that they should get on well together: fortunately Eddie and I made a good team.

He was a Bevin Boy, the first I had ever worked with, and was cable dragger himself for a year before taking over on the tadger. Though we had both been directed into the pits this was about the only thing we had in common. Whereas I was a country bumpkin, he was a sharp-eyed quick-witted city dweller who could talk the hind leg off a donkey. No faceman ever got the better of an argument with him! The reason he and I worked well together was that our personalities seemed to complement each other, his urban brashness offsetting my rustic caution and vice versa.

Eddie had a golden rule, a guiding star, which influenced his conduct down the pit. This was to get into the pit bottom promptly at three o'clock at the end of each shift. Being a day traveller he had to catch a bus from outside the pithead baths at 3.45 p.m. in order to reach home twenty miles away. Unless he was on one of the first cages up he missed the bus and was unable to get home at a reasonable hour. Thus during the last hour of the shift Eddie became like a man possessed. No matter how many obstacles beset us nothing could hold him back once he had that three o'clock glint in his eye. I was equally glad to get up the pit early though I often used to wonder whether it was worth while in view of the mad chase that inevitably preceded it.

Our practice was to get to the bottom of the face as soon as possible after two o'clock without bothering to coil up the cable as we went along. On reaching the bottom we sat straddled one behind the other, steadied ourselves against a firm tree and pulled down the cable, in-out, in-out, like a rowing crew. However the cable did not always come willingly. By late afternoon a forest of foresets and mainsets had been erected and in our hurry to get down the face we often got the cable looped round a tree. If this happened we had to cart the cumbersome tadger back up the face to where we had gone wrong and unloop the cable from around the offending tree. Occasionally we pulled so hard at the cable that we collapsed the tree, much to the annoyance of the faceman who had erected it, though it saved us another upward journey. If they had finished work and were in a playful mood the facemen, who knew perfectly well why we were in such a hurry, tried to frustrate us either by sitting on the cable or pulling against us, but whatever they did they never stopped us for long: Eddie saw to that.

After removing the tadger and cable into the security of the middle road Eddie and I then had the hazardous adventure of sneaking out to the pit bottom without being spotted by the Firemen, District Fireman or Overman. The shift ended officially at three o'clock when the banksmen rang down the shaft a special signal consisting of two long blasts followed by three short ones. This signal, known as 'lillicock', was flashed along the bell wires of all the underground districts notifying the workers that they could now go home. As you were allowed to walk into work in the colliery's time at the start of the shift you were expected to walk out in your own time after the shift, and it was strictly against the rules to leave your post till lillicock had rung even though you might have finished the job you had been told to do.

By early 1947 the South Shallow face had advanced a good mile from the pit bottom and it took about twenty minutes to walk out by which time a huge queue had assembled at the bottom of the shaft. After waiting ten minutes or more in the queue it was gone half past three before you finally reached the surface. Such delay was inconceivable to Eddie and me: so each day we smuggled ourselves off the face before time, provided of course we were no longer required on the face. Normally the tadger man was not in demand towards the end of the shift, all the coal having then been fired.

We were handicapped by our lamps which could be seen from a long distance in the dark but the odds were that we saw the gaffers' lamps first, particularly as they carried the unmistakable shinies and safeties. In the event of running into gaffers we either had to double back as quickly as possible or try our luck at hiding. Several times Eddie and I lay curled up in a manhole, hardly daring to breathe while the silver rays of the gaffers' lamps flashed up and down outside. On one occasion, when I weakly chose to give myself up rather than risk hiding, I gazed aghast as the Overman stood threatening to report me for misconduct, at the same time spitting his tobacco juice into the tub in which Eddie was concealed! As a rule though we reached the approaches to the pit bottom without any trouble.

Because the men working in the pit bottom kept fairly clean we had to be careful not to show our black faces among all the white ones or this would have given us away immediately to any gaffer on the prowl: so we lay low in the shadowy road ends opening into the main haulage road and waited for lillicock to ring. When this happened an amazing transformation took place. Suddenly out of nowhere sprang scores of miners and Bevin Boys who like us had been quietly creeping up on the pit bottom from districts all over the pit. The main haulage road, which a moment before had been deserted, swarmed with an awesome stampede as old men, young men, tall men and short men raced their way, shoving and kicking, down the last hundred yards to the base of the shaft, where the cage was waiting to begin its upward journeys. If anyone fell he was instantly trampled on, or if he dropped his lamp or helmet he had no chance to retrieve it but was hustled forward by the inexorable thrust from behind. To the twenty or so victors of this bizarre marathon – sometimes they included Eddie and me – went the privilege of the first journey up the shaft into the daylight, a soaring flight that never lost its thrill no matter how often you did it.

At the hostel a great change was taking place but not, alas, for the better. During the closing months of 1946 the number of residents had dwindled to not more than a hundred, the sole survivors of the original five hundred Bevin Boys. This had been an idyllic time at Wimblebury: with so few to be catered for the food was excellent, the hostel was kept spotlessly clean, the number of girls on the staff was almost sufficient to go round, and manager, staff and residents lived like one large family.

Then came the Celtic invasion! On the crags above the hostel huge excavators commenced burrowing for opencast coal – and wretched dismal grey stuff it was, too – most of the men employed on this large-scale project being Irish. From a Ministerial point of view it was a shrewd undertaking, with imported workers to conserve home labour and a half empty hostel, which hadn't been paying for years, on hand to put them in. Thus during the early weeks of 1947 there was a big influx of Irish workers at the hostel and soon the number of residents was not far from full strength.

Soon too the pleasant family atmosphere at Wimblebury Hostel had utterly disappeared.

There were soup trails down the floor, ponds of gravy on the tables, opencast mud on the chairs, black high tide marks at various levels on the wash basins and choked lavatories which took an engineering feat to flush. On Saturday evenings the odour of drink hung heavily on the air, angry voices echoed in disputation, loud crashes went bump in the night, and on Sunday mornings the corridors crunched with glass from broken windows and bristled with the remnants of wooden beds. Yet we managed to survive the ordeal which was more than many of the newcomers did, the weekend riots resulting in a stream of evictions for damage. One weekend a whole dormitory of twelve was evicted after an orgy at the end of which not one of the dormitory's fittings remained intact.

As a protective measure the few Bevin Boys left at the hostel banded together in the same dormitories and when a bed fell vacant hastily filled it with a person of their own choosing. Fortunately the staff still clung to us, perhaps as symbols of the happy days that had gone, and we were not often conscious of being in a minority. But to our dismay our old friends on the staff were presently replaced by thrush-voiced Irish colleens, presumably imported to make their compatriots feel more at home. At first we were inclined to feel indignant about this but the newcomers were so delightful with their lucid eyes and honeyed brogue that we soon gave in and were as ready as the Irishmen to compete for their affections.

Nationalisation of the mining industry was dealt a severe blow by the rigorous winter of 1946/7 which aggravated the already critical shortage of coal supplies. Several light falls of snow during the early part of February were followed by that amazing blizzard which overnight left the entire country snow-bound and paralysed. The afternoon workers at Littleton Colliery, ascending the pit at eleven o'clock when the blizzard was at its height, were obliged to sleep the night in the canteen when their bus failed to collect them after being stranded in a drift, where it remained for many days.

On the morning after the blizzard we woke on Cannock Chase to a fantastic new world where all the sharp edges of the landscape had been rounded off by buxom white billows of snow. Roads had vanished; drifts crept to the tops of telegraph poles and buildings shivered under glittering garments of ice. Since only the Bevin Boys working at pits in the immediate vicinity of the hostel were able to get to work, the rest of us set to work clearing the road to the hostel to ensure the delivery of supplies.

For several weeks the temperature rarely rose above freezing point and the landscape lay buried under its thick eiderdown of snow, whose whiteness got steadily grubbier from the smoky breath of colliery chimneys. The hostel heating system, never a happy arrangement, was entirely inadequate for such weather and it became almost as cold inside as out. In the dormitories the hot water pipes were suspended round the ceiling so that any heat provided went straight up through the roof: it seemed incredible that the architects should have ignored the simple basic fact that heat went up and not down. Each evening we sat embracing radiators in the welfare block till it was time to retire to our frigid beds; my face flannel and soap froze nightly in the dish, and with all the windows firmly shut no fresh air got into the room with the result that in the morning our dormitory of twelve stank.

After a couple of days it became possible to reach Littleton Colliery again by a détour which doubled the normal travelling distance. As a rule, by leaving the hostel at 6.20 a.m. you could reach the colliery by 6.45 but now a totally new system was evolved.

Having made up your mind to go to work, which was not easy when your bed was just getting warm, you proceeded to the bus stop and took your place in the queue as early as possible before 5.50, this being the time when the first bus was due. After a wait of up to three quarters of an hour, the bus appeared – whether it was the 5.50, the 6.5 or the 6.20 was uncertain – and if you were fortunate enough to get on board, for even on these abnormal mornings the brassy-voiced bus conductresses would not allow more than the regulation five standing, you completed the first half of the journey by 6.40. Then followed another wait of possibly half an hour for the next bus connection, which did not get you to the colliery until after the half past seven hooter had gone. Thus over an hour and a half was spent in travelling to work, a distance of only four or five miles as the crow flew, though it of course did not have six foot deep snow drifts to contend with.

The return journey in the afternoon was less arduous though it was frustrating to have to stand shivering in a bus queue after taking a hot shower and getting thoroughly warmed up for the evening. And as if things weren't bad enough, when a nearby school emptied at a quarter to four the queue was subjected to a cannonade of snowballs from all the children of the neighbourhood, who seemed fiendishly determined to provoke the queuers into breaking formation to retaliate and thus forfeit their positions.

On my first day back at the pit it was eight o'clock before I had changed into my pit clothes and collected my check, half an hour after the last cage of riders had descended. With so much clearance work to be done above ground the Manager decided that all those unavoidably late should be given jobs on the Bank though paid their usual underground rate, so with thirty or forty other miners and Bevin Boys I was set to work shifting the snow. Never before had the warm underground life so appealed to me! For the first time I had been genuinely relishing going below but instead I had been thrust almost naked into the snow and ice of the cruellest winter of the half century.

My outfit consisted of a collarless cotton shirt, a jacket minus a sleeve, trousers with a doubtful seat and no knees, old socks with holes in them and pit boots that were falling apart: excellent underground wear but hardly the thing for outdoors. My job was helping a couple of well clad banksmen to uncover and restack steel trees: long, smooth, ice-covered steel trees that benumbed the hands and grated the teeth as they crashed together with dreadful metallic discord. From time to time we warmed ourselves gratefully in front of one of the open braziers which dotted the pithead, their bright flames blossoming like orange flowers in the drab whiteness, but for most of this harrowing day my hands and feet were as dead as doornails.

The next morning I came to work armed with an old mackintosh, waistcoat, vest, extra socks and a pair of gloves, but this time we were sent below. Though the gaffers were as reluctant as ever to halt the drawing it was arranged that at eight o'clock a couple of cage runs should be made to get the latecomers below; mopping up on the bank had for the most part been completed and many of the men who had been kept on top were now needed below.

The shaft of No. 3 Pit was very damp, moisture continually seeping through its brick walls, and as a result of the hard frost it became icebound. As this was considered serious two tubs of blazing coal were stationed at the top of the shaft all through the day, the warm air being drawn down with the ventilation current and thawing the ice from the walls. This meant that moisture fell down the shaft like heavy rain and the cage emerged dripping from each run. The onsetter in the pit bottom, who pushed the loaded tubs on to the cage, had a most miserable job and though wrapped in oilskins got well and truly soaked by the end of the shift.

During the cold spell homes and factories throughout the country underwent a serious fuel shortage; the B.B.C. reduced its programmes to conserve power, and extensive gas and electricity cuts took place. When an urgent appeal was made by the Government for miners to step up coal output the Littleton men responded magnificently; there were record attendances on Saturdays as well as on other weekdays and many of the men also worked on Sundays. It is unlikely that their response would have been so great had the mines not belonged to the nation.

For weeks the weather showed no signs of improving and it became hard to imagine the landscape without snow or the buses ever running to time again. Then late one evening as we were going to bed the arrival of a thaw was heralded by a tell-tale trickle under the dormitory door, and soon the room was under water again. As we had now got used to the invading stream we were determined not to let it interfere with our night's rest, so after hanging the floor mats on the hot water pipes, putting our boots on the window sills and emptying the bottom shelves of our lockers, we went off to sleep with the water, now a foot high, lapping round the legs of our beds.

After this the thaw set in quickly; the landscape shook off its snowy covering, green turf thrust in widening patches through the white crust, rivulets chattered down the hill paths and the valley stream thundered under the road bridge. The hard winter was ending at last.

With the South Shallow menaced by the roll special teams were opening up a new face at the entrance to the district, only a short distance from the pit bottom. This was to ensure that when the inevitable happened and the roll prevented any further drawing off the old face the men would have other work to move to without delay.

It was during March that the roll entered the top side of the face, first appearing opposite the junction of the middle road. As it was here that the scraper chain descending the face emptied into the main conveyor belt travelling to the loader it was essential that this all important junction should not be obstructed. Thus the gaffers spared no effort to see that the bottom end was drawn off as effectively as possible each day despite the contortions in the seam caused by the roll. As the coal cutter could not get under the roll the affected area was drawn off entirely by pick and shovel, extra labour being allocated to the regular facemen.

As a result of their efforts this particular battle with the roll was won. Within a couple of weeks it had moved away from the bottom end, which then reverted to its normal height; but though the road junction had been saved, the stents above it were now in jeopardy with the roof lowering to within two feet of the floor. This constricted the air current up the face so that it emerged from under the roll like a tornado, sending up clouds of dust. The atmosphere was so choking that the men working immediately above the roll were given masks to wear.

Soon it was impossible to draw off the stents in which the roll was located, but goaded by the fact that further up the face were twenty or more good stents waiting to be tapped the gaffers gave orders for a short tunnel to be driven through the roll, big enough to take a steep metal chute which could then continue to feed the main conveyor belt in the middle road. This meant that the only way to get up the face from the middle road was to wriggle up this tunnel to where the face assumed its normal height.

Once the shift had started this chute became impassable for long periods, so Eddie and I could no longer have our snaps in the middle road but had to take our sandwiches on the face with us. Before we learnt to do this a snapping occurred when we were both stranded on the face with our snaps still in our jacket pockets in the middle road. Fortunately one of the Deputy Firemen came to our rescue. Kneeling at the top of the chute, he shouted to those below that he was going to lower down his cable and that he wanted them to tie Eddie's snap and mine to the end of it so that he could haul these up to us. This plan proved a complete success and Eddie and I were soon eating our sandwiches.

Then a faint voice at the other end of the chute called up to the Fireman, 'What about yours, Bert?'

Bert shouted back, 'It doesn't matter about mine, mate.'

'I can get it for you all right, Bert,' the voice at the other end persisted.

Bert then replied, rather sadly, 'It's no use, mate. My teeth are down there as well.'

But our Good Samaritan below was ready for any emergency and Bert soon had both his snap and his false teeth dangling on the end of his line.

Owing to the awkward conditions created by the roll Eddie and I were finding it increasingly difficult to get away before three o'clock each day. Not only were the men working later, thus requiring us to remain to drill shot holes, but at the end of each shift we had the appalling task of lowering the tadger, the cable and ourselves down the chute into the middle road. Little wonder that Eddie's eyes turned eagerly towards the new face which was within two minutes' run of the pit bottom, and when it was reported that a tadger man was wanted on this face he was the first to grab the job.

After he had gone conditions on the old face got so bad that it was impossible to draw off each shift. The District Fireman was the next to go to the new district; he was followed soon afterwards by most of the Deputy Firemen and contract men, till only six of the older facemen and myself, now in sole charge of the tadger, were left behind on the dying South Shallow face.

CHAPTER ELEVEN

The Slave Market

IN MAY 1947 a five day working week was introduced in the coal mining industry. At a time when the country was calling for greater coal output this may have seemed unwarranted, but it was in fact a shrewd gesture on the part of the National Coal Board. Of course their chief motive was to see that the miners got the shorter working week that they deserved but the Board must also have realised that the new arrangement would do much to reduce absenteeism.

Since the end of the war absenteeism had been a growing problem on Cannock Chase, particularly on Saturdays. The men had responded well during the fuel crisis earlier in the year but had come to work less regularly since then. Owing to the unexpected absence of key workers on various days the District Firemen had great difficulty in running their districts efficiently: to fill up the labour gaps on the face and in the haulage roads they had to keep drawing on a reserve pool of experienced workers who would have been much better employed in regular jobs of their own.

The introduction of a five day week gave the National Coal Board an opportunity to hit back at absenteeism. They could not force the men to come to work but by dispensing with the Saturday shift, which was virtually useless anyway, they could at least guarantee a good attendance on the other days. This was by giving the men their Saturday pay in the form of a bonus but only on condition they had worked all the other five shifts.

It was obvious that a man was going to think twice before taking a day off if he stood to lose two shifts' wages which in the case of contract men meant reducing his wage packet by at least £2. 10s. I know that in my own case it had a very beneficial effect on attendance. After the second week in May I was paid the usual company rate for five shifts with an additional bonus of eleven shillings and sixpence in lieu of Saturday pay. Miners who still wished to work on Saturdays or Sundays were allowed to do so provided they had already worked the other five shifts.

On the South Shallow face I had now become the combined tadger man and cable dragger though I was still paid the company rate. To be honest I had so little work to do that I did not merit contract pay. With only six facemen engaged on drawing I had scarcely more than a dozen shot holes to drill per shift. The face was drawn off in stages, it taking three or four shifts to complete the process. The men started with the top six stents and gradually worked their way down to the roll.

The greatest hardship for me was dragging the tadger on and off the face at the beginning and end of each shift. Since the tadger was kept in the middle road I was obliged to collect it from there in the morning and take it back in the afternoon which meant going up and down the chute each shift. Luckily for them the facemen had no particular cause to use the middle road and came in by the top road in order to avoid negotiating the chute, which was always an uncomfortable business.

The worst thing that could happen when you were inside the chute was for someone to start the scraper chain on the face with the result that it began emptying coal down on top of you. The only remedy then was to beat a hasty exit either up or down, whichever was the nearest way. On one occasion I was struggling with the tadger halfway up the chute when I saw a pair of legs illumined at the top, clumsily descending and bringing down a quantity of loose coal with them.

'Get back you fool!' I yelled, as the lumps bounced down at me. 'Can't you see there's someone down here? Haven't you got any bloody eyes in your head?'

I noted with satisfaction that the legs quickly retreated but was disconcerted on reaching the top to find that they belonged to my old enemy the Under Manager.

'I'm sorry,' I said. 'I didn't know it was you.'

'That's all right, lad,' he said amicably. 'Carry on. You're doing a good job.' The feud was over at last.

To take the tadger off the face at the end of the shift I used to let it slide down the chute to the man at the bottom, whom I had previously warned to be ready to catch it. I tried getting down this way myself once but never again! I whizzed down the chute, shot on to the main conveyor belt and was rapidly borne off into the darkness, leaving my helmet and lamp behind. Fortunately on recovering from the shock of my sudden arrival the man at the bottom of the chute hung on to the bell wire till the belt stopped, otherwise I would probably have gone over the loader and added my special contribution to Littleton output.

If the men were working in the top stents I had a long journey up the face after crawling through the chute. Apart from the tadger I also carried two drills, one six feet long and the other four feet. I threw these ahead of me like javelins, dragged the tadger up to where they had fallen and then pulled up the slack cable, repeating this process till my upward journey was completed. On my belt I carried a leather pouch containing three sharp metal bits, collected on the Bank each morning; on reaching the men I took a bit from the pouch and fastened it with a cotter pin to the end of the drill, which was then ready for use. At the end of the shift I handed in the pouch, the bits being re-sharpened overnight ready to be collected the following morning.

Drilling the shot holes was not a new experience because I had done it occasionally while working with Eddie. After fitting the drill into the nozzle of the tadger you gripped the side handles, applied the switch – located inside one of the handles – and directed the whirring drill into the coal, whichever way you wanted it to go. The hardest holes to drill were those in the tops, where the tadger, a heavy instrument, had to be raised and operated above your head. Another tricky manoeuvre was drilling next to a shot hole that had failed to go off when detonated. The second hole had to be drilled as close as possible to the first one but did not have to run into it otherwise the drill might touch and set off the undetonated charge.

In the South Shallow these days there was none of the bustle of a thriving district. With such an awkward system of drawing there were regular breakdowns, each shift being interrupted by long periods of deep quiet as a lone mechanic laboured to repair broken machinery or a grumbling Fireman struggled to free the coal-blocked chute. Such interruptions did not bring the District Fireman or Overman racing in, as they would have done in the old days, to find out what was holding things up. The new district now had the priority treatment. The old district was moribund and everyone knew it. It was only a question of how much longer it could last out.

During breakdowns the six veteran facemen whom I served as tadger man used to squat down and wait till the chain started up again. They were gentler and more characterful than the younger miners. They had been through a lot and their lined faces showed it. Crouched in the eerie glow of the lamps they looked like gnomes in a magic circle: a resemblance enhanced by the peculiar headgear, relics of caps and bonnets of yesteryear that most of them wore to keep out the dust. To listen to them holding forth in the underground idiom, particularly when relating yarns, was fascinating. The following was one of the tales I was told, though lacking its colloquial embroidery it seems a shadow of the original.

I had just bought a new tin water bottle, a 'clock' bottle as it was called because it was circular like a clock's dial. I held it up to one of the facemen, its brand new surface gleaming in the lamplight. 'Not bad, eh?' I said.

'Wouldn't bring one of them down the pit not if you was to pay me,' he retorted.

'Why not?' I asked.

'Because I don't trust 'em,' he replied. He seemed to sense another 'Why?' coming because before I could interrupt he added, 'If you'd had the experience I had with one of them things you wouldn't neither.'

'What happened, then?' I said.

He obviously wanted to tell me but hesitated for a moment as if first getting the facts straight in his head. Then he went on, 'Well, I had one of them tin bottles meself once. It was a long time ago, mind, before you was thought of, and I warn't workin' at this pit then. I had a stent on a gain face down that fair-sized colliery t'other side of Cannock.

'I used to take the bottle down with me each morning with me bread in a tin so as the moggies shouldn't get at it. Well, one shift I goes to get a drink and finds that the cork's gone off the top of me bottle. At first I thought I must've knocked it off walkin' in but when I shook the bottle I could hear the damn thing rattlin' inside so I reckoned I must have pushed it in too far.

'I got hold of some paper and stuffed up the neck with it and then went back to me work thinkin' no more about it. We didn't have any baths in them days and I used to go home at night in me black, taking the bottle with me. Well, you know what a game it is to get a cork from inside a bottle, so when I got hold of another cork I didn't moither meself about getting t'other one out.

'I used to find that tin bottle very handy. Each night I'd go down to the pub and have a pint: then I'd have the bottle filled up and bring back some beer to have with me supper. Well, it would be about a fortnight later when I come back from the pit one afternoon feelin' real bad. There was a lot of 'flu about and I reckoned I had a touch of it. I didn't feel like going out to the pub but all the same I wanted a drop of beer with me supper, so I sent the old woman out with the bottle.

'When she come back she said to me, "Dad, you've got a cork inside that bottle." I said I knew I had and that it had been there the best part of a fortnight but she said she wouldn't rest till she'd got it out – you know what women are! – so I emptied out the beer and gave her the bottle. She stood it on the table, looped a piece of string and lowered it inside and started to fish around.

'She'd been at it the best part of half an hour and I was gettin' real fed up when she shouts, "I've got it, Dad!" and starts drawin' it through the neck of the bottle. But as it dropped on the table she suddenly let out a scream ; it wasn't no cork inside the bottle but a dead moggy what must've got in after the cork had fallen out!'

The old man paused after this: his voice had been rising but now it dropped to a whisper. 'Well, I went out in the backyard,' he said, 'and I brought up me tea and I brought up me snap and I reckon I brought up me breakfast as well but I only wished to 'eaven I could have brought up every drop I'd had out of that bottle in the past fortnight.'

Then searching the pockets of his jacket he pulled out what appeared to be an old whisky bottle. 'And that's why I always brings a glass bottle down the pit with me,' he said, 'because nothing can get inside of it without me knowing what it is!'

With such frequent breakdowns the men were always behind with their work and I rarely got into the pit bottom before half past three despite running all the way. Far more mishaps befell me during those hectic races down the long dusty tunnels to the pit bottom than when I was at work on the face. With no one ahead to shout 'Feet' or 'Head' I was forever falling over haulage gear in the road, or colliding with slobs projecting from the roof, thereby seeing red, white and blue stars in the otherwise starless darkness. My shirt was wet with sweat by the time I reached the pit bottom and was still damp when I came to put it on in the baths next morning, thus giving a sour clammy start to the day.

However I was not only perspiring below ground. Things were also getting hot on top. After a freezing winter we were now getting a scorching summer. Day after day the sun blazed down on the tin roofs of the hostel turning the dormitories, which earlier in the year had been refrigerators, into ovens. The heat indoors was stifling; windows were flung open wide, and music from radios drifted out on the hot syrupy air. All the valley was becalmed; only on the crags of the moor could a faint stirring of wind be felt. In the late afternoons the yellow grass outside the dormitories was littered with the naked bodies of sunbathers out to regain a dose of the sunshine they had lost at work during the day, while the nights were spent alternately wincing from sunburn or searching for insects, hundreds of which crawled through the open windows into the beds.

At the beginning of September I celebrated my twenty first birthday though it was not a particularly joyful occasion. I was at work during the day and there was no chance of holding a party in the evening because all the other members of my dormitory were working on the afternoon shift from 3 to 10.30 p.m. This was known as the old man's shift because life consisted almost entirely of working and sleeping. It was unnecessary to get up till after nine o'clock in the morning – or even later if you felt like missing breakfast – but the fact that you had to report for work at three ruled out any evening pleasures such as beer drinking or cinema going. However the hours were very pleasant and my dormitory mates had willingly accepted or even volunteered for afternoons. I might have done so myself but there was no way of getting back from Littleton at a late hour.

Though I could not have a party I was determined not to let my coming of age pass unobserved. I therefore decided to obtain twelve bottles of beer and conceal one in each of the dormitory beds so that when the lads came back at about 11.30 p.m. we could have a nocturnal celebration. The trouble was that intoxicants were forbidden at the hostel.

Nevertheless I arranged with the proprietor of the off-licence in Wimblebury village to collect twelve bottles of beer from him at nine o'clock, just as dusk was falling. Since I did not wish to be seen coming from the shop with a loaded case or haversack I decided to smuggle the bottles into the hostel by concealing them in my thick ex-A.R.P. coat, which had several commodious pockets. When the time came I donned this coat and embarked on my mission. As it was a sultry evening my muffled appearance must have caused much head shaking among the shirt-sleeved residents of Wimblebury.

The proprietor of the shop was fascinated as I stowed the bottles in various corners of my person and helpfully opened the door for me as I tottered out on the pavement, nearly double my normal girth. With each step forward there was a clinking of bottles and I had to perform remarkable contortions to prevent those bottles less securely stowed from slipping. To my relief however the dormitory was reached without incident and the bottles were safely laid between the sheets of the twelve beds.

Even then my plans went awry. After waiting up till after eleven I got into bed, intending to continue waiting there, but the inevitable happened. I dozed off and when the others came in they found their host fast asleep. Naturally they tried to wake me to drink my health but were drowsily, grumpily told to shut up and let a man sleep, which they obligingly did.

Soon after my twenty first birthday the South Shallow district was closed down. Far from diminishing, the roll had continued to worsen till it was no longer possible to operate a chute through it. Thus the essential link between the scraper chain descending the face and the main conveyor belt in the middle road could no longer be maintained with the result that all drawing ceased. The facemen were given the job of stacking off the face with sand to prevent combustion; the mechanics set to work dismantling the machinery and soon the South Shallow was nothing more than a forgotten catacomb, deserted, silent and dead.

After the closing of the South Shallow I saw more of No. 3 Pit in two weeks than I had done in all my previous three years at the colliery, my third anniversary as a Bevin Boy having now arrived. Out of a job and with my district shut down I became a member of what I used to regard as the slave market. Having no District Fireman to report to I stood each morning in the pit bottom with a number of other similarly placed persons while the District Firemen of the various districts eyed us up and down, deciding whether we were suitable or strong enough for any of the jobs they wanted filled.

I always hoped that the District Fireman of the old South Shallow who had come to my rescue once before, would find a job for me on the new district that had been opened out but it appeared he had too many men in his book already. I certainly knew the districts I didn't want: Fifty five's for instance, which was over two miles' hiking distance away, and Forty nine's, where the face yielded the best coal in the pit but was only three feet high.

When the District Firemen of these districts glanced in my direction I made sure I was tying my bootlace or looking as though I hadn't an ounce of strength in me.

At first I was sent to a heading where all the haulage work had to be done manually. For three days several of us mauled away, doing the donkey work as the miners called it, till machinery was provided to do the job: then our services were no longer required. The next day I went as mate to a bricklayer, who travelled around, building or reinforcing the walls of road junctions. The following morning however his regular mate returned, and I was sent to work in the main haulage road of the North Shallow, rival district to the old South Shallow though not a patch on it in my estimation.

My performance during this shift was the most disastrous of my career as a Bevin Boy. I succeeded in nothing less than holding up the work of the entire district for almost an hour.

The truth was that I was not cut out to be a haulage hand. I didn't have the quickness of mind or adroitness of hand essential for the job. I had realised this as far back as my days at the training centre when we were first taught how to clip and unclip tubs to a moving rope, and it had always been a relief to me that I had never been directed to haulage work. On this particular day however I had no alternative but to take it though I approached the task with justifiable foreboding.

My instructions were to take up a solitary station at a bend in the main haulage road about midway between the loader and the pit bottom. I had to keep an eye on the journeys of full tubs coming out and empty tubs going in; if any of the tubs showed signs of coming off the track it was my job to get them back on again. As haulage jobs went it was just about the easiest you could get.

At first all went well for the simple reason that none of the tubs were off the track, but after about an hour a journey of empties came along in which one of the centre tubs in a line of about fifteen was dragging along with its two rear wheels off the rails. Lifting an empty tub back on to the track was a simple task, or so it appeared when other people did it: all they did was lift and twist without bothering to stop the moving rope, which was something you should never do if you could avoid it.

Unfortunately when I tried lifting on this tub I only succeeded in getting the front wheels off the track as well as the rear ones.

Further efforts to correct the situation resulted in a second tub being derailed, which pulled off a third and a fourth. With nervous sweat sprouting from my forehead I rushed anxiously to the opposite wall to pull the bell wire to stop the rope.

However a journey of full tubs from the loader was then travelling along the track between me and the bell wire. I tried reaching over the top of them to pull the wire but calamitously dropped my handlamp, which provided the only light there was. When this happened I became panic stricken. I couldn't see what I was doing or what was happening around me, my lamp being concealed under the journey of loaded tubs passing over it. Before I dropped my lamp nearly half the journey of empty tubs had come off the track and swung across the road towards the loaded journey.

As the two journeys tangled together in the pitch darkness there was a dreadful banging of metal followed by a tremendous crash of timber and débris, the cause of which I could not at that time imagine. I still groped desperately for the bell wire but without success: to my relief, however, the moving rope suddenly came to a halt. It transpired that the driver in the motor house half a mile away had become so alarmed by the tension of the rope that he stopped the motor for an investigation to be made.

With everything brought to a standstill I was able to retrieve my lamp and survey what had happened. I trembled at what I saw! The collision of the empty tubs with the full ones had resulted in several of the latter tipping over and spilling their contents across the road. But worse still, one of the full tubs which had been derailed had jammed against an arched girder of the roof and demolished it, bringing down a quantity of overhead timber and rock. I could scarcely believe that I alone could have been responsible for such a disaster.

I wished myself a thousand miles away as I saw pinpricks of lights approaching: the handlamps of other haulage workers coming to see what the trouble was. The gravity of the mishap was indicated by the men's reaction when they reached the scene. They neither swore nor expostulated, as I expected – even hoped they would. They just stood almost silent. 'Well, this is a tidy mess!' said one in an awed voice. 'We'm doin' all right here!' said another.

My worst moment came when the flashing beams of a shiny proclaimed the arrival of the District Fireman who had booked me for the job that morning. I expected him to thunder abuse at me but he seemed just as taken aback by the catastrophe as the other men. He simply said to me, quietly, 'Get along to the loader and find yourself a job there. I think you've done enough out here for one day.' I was not even to be given the privilege of helping to clear up my own mess.

Nearly an hour went by before the road had been cleared and drawing recommenced, during which time scores of men all over the district were kept idle. It was the last time I was ever given a job in the North Shallow.

The following Monday morning, despite my efforts to escape his notice, the District Fireman of Forty nine's beckoned me over and gave me a job in his district. I almost shed tears when he told me it would be cleaning out the tension end. After a long walk I found myself in the middle road of Forty nine's, obtained a shovel and crawled on to the face. Though perfectly level the face was only about three feet high: at that time of the morning with the coal piled up to the roof it looked even less. The only way I could reach the tension end was by crawling along the rubber conveyor belt, which had a space of about two feet between it and the roof. As the seam was flat a belt was used to take the coal to the middle road instead of a scraper chain.

Owing to the narrowness of the seam the stents had to be larger to give the facemen an adequate cubic area of coal to remove, and the face seemed an extraordinary length. I crawled along, scraping my back on the roof and poking the shovel handle in my eyes, till I reached the tension end, then spent the rest of the shift at my old game of shovelling slack, though the outpour was not so great as it had been on a sloping face. I tried to shovel kneeling, reclining on my side and lying flat on my stomach but could not get comfortable in any position. I wondered how I could have endured such a monotonous job for so long on the South Shallow when the hours now seemed to dawdle past.

By the end of the week it was apparent that the District Fireman of Forty nine's regarded me as his regular man at the tension end. I had tried coming down the pit as late as possible in the hope that he might have given the job to someone else but this ruse failed to work. The last straw occurred when I was given a pair of knee pads to protect me when kneeling down to shovel: a sure sign that my job was regarded as a permanency. This was a prospect I simply could not endure. It was not the lowness of the roof that bothered me or the long distance to be walked in; it was the dreariness of the work. I felt I had done enough tension end shovelling to last me a life-time. As far as I could see there was only one way out and that was to stay away from work till someone else had been broken in as the new tension end man on Forty nine's. With this in mind I went off without consulting anyone for a fortnight's holiday, youth hostelling in Devonshire.

While on holiday I learnt a lesson that anyone proposing to travel on his own should remember. Towards the end of the first week I set out to hike across a desolate stretch of Dartmoor. When I had reached the loneliest, bleakest part of my journey a thick mist descended, blotting out the landscape, and I became lost. While sheltering against a rock, waiting in vain for the mist to lift, a frightening thought occurred to me. If I were to stay lost or break a leg or be trapped in a bog or pit, no one in the whole world would know where I was or even care for at least four to six weeks. Before going away I had not told my father what I was doing because I knew that absenting myself from work would displease him. I had not told the colliery for obvious reasons; the other members of my dormitory knew I was going but did not know where. If I failed to return to the hostel, neither the colliery nor my dormitory mates would take this amiss since they would assume that like various other Bevin Boys I had decided to abscond.

To my shame I did not write home more than once a month or even longer, so my father would not grow concerned regarding my whereabouts till at least four weeks had passed. And as I was hiking from hostel to hostel without booking in advance no one would be expecting me to arrive that evening. My predicament suddenly became so unnerving that rather than go on waiting in suspense I pushed ahead, hoping for the best. Fortunately I struck a track from a disused quarry which led me off the moor into clear air at almost exactly the same point from which I had started. After this experience I vowed that I would never go anywhere in the wilds again without at least one person knowing where I was.

Contemptible though it may have been, my deliberate absence from work achieved its desired result for when I returned after a fortnight the District Fireman of Forty nine's ignored me, having found someone else to install at the tension end. By great good luck the District Fireman who had employed me on the South

Shallow saw me loitering in the slave market and signed me up for a job that had then come vacant on his new district. Of course Eddie had been tadger man on the face there for a couple of months, but during that time had found a new mate so there was no chance of my working with him again.

Instead I was directed to the loader, not a location I would normally have enjoyed though it seemed like paradise after some of the other places I had encountered during my travels around No. 3 Pit. My job was to push the empty tubs under the end of the conveyor belt to catch the coal as it tumbled off. As each tub filled up it was shoved away by another empty pushed into it from behind. The loading routine was conducted at a fast pace throughout the day though towards the end of the shift, when the facemen were finishing off or setting up roof supports, there was less coal coming along the belt and thus less shoving of tubs to be done.

The new district had quickly become the major productive district of No. 3 Pit, a distinction once held by the South Shallow, and – marvellous to relate – the loader was manned entirely by Bevin Boys. There were about six of us working there, a congregation of conscripts unheard of in the old days. We had our own Bevin Boy foreman and took our duties very seriously. If the belt came to a standstill or failed to deliver any coal we were the first to yell for drawing to resume instantly. Perhaps the most significant development lay in the changed attitude towards us of the gaffers and miners. They no longer treated us as a burden or a joke but looked upon us as responsible workers whom they could trust. Though the Bevin Boy scheme might only have been a qualified success the majority of those lads who finished their time proved themselves useful in a variety of jobs. Indeed I suspected the gaffers were beginning to worry about how they were going to replace us when our release came through. Fortunately a solution to their problem was on hand.

At the hostel there was once more plenty of accommodation available. The imported Irish workers had not proved a success; many had gone away, either voluntarily or otherwise, and the number of residents had again dwindled to less than two hundred. Thus, with the stroke of an official pen, Wimblebury Hostel became a sanctuary for Displaced Persons, the harassed and homeless of Europe.

During its four years of existence the hostel had housed all manner of people. The Bevin Boys had been an odd assortment, mixing West Country farmers' boys with Black Country foundry workers; then there had been the Irishmen with their exuberant brogue and blarney, but never had the hostel welcomed a more diverse collection of humanity than that now crowding through its portals. There were Czechs, Poles, Estonians, Latvians, Lithuanians – soon almost every European nationality was represented on the register. They were all male mining volunteers who soon made their presence felt underground. By this time the miners, who had once worked as an isolated clan, had grown accustomed to unexpected workmates but at least they and the Bevin Boys had spoken the same language. Now they had to get used to working with, say, some burly Lithuanian, whose nodding grin was intended to offset the fact that his knowledge of English began and ended with 'Good morning, how are you?' Optimistically the miners murmured, 'Maybe they'll send down chorus girls next!'

The D.Ps. were admirably behaved though not over keen to mix with the 'foreign' English residents at the hostel. Most of them could not speak or read English and hostel notices had to be printed in several languages. Naturally there were often misunderstandings over the purchase of meal tickets or other transactions and soon the Irish colleens who had replaced the English staff were themselves replaced by female D.Ps. This had a pronounced effect on the cooking which became East European in flavour and slightly too greasy for Bevin Boy palates. The mail lists posted up on the hostel noticeboard each day had a remarkably cosmopolitan air, reading something like this:

Bienkiewicz
Brachmanski
Brown
Cieslewicz
Finnegan
Hooper
Janovskis
Konstantinowicz
Murphy
O'Reilly
Poloczek
Smith, etc.

The hostel population became composed of approximately 50 per cent D.Ps., 30 per cent Irish workers, and 20 per cent Bevin Boys. The small percentage of Bevin Boys was however soon to disappear. Slowly but not entirely unnoticed the demob. group numbers had mounted till at last the unbelievable happened and a Bevin Boy received his official release papers. After this the Bevin Boys at the hostel and at the pit began disappearing, one by one, till none was left on Cannock Chase.

One of the first to go from Littleton was Eddie's mate, who, though he had not been at the pit as long as most of us, was an older man and therefore in a lower release group. When he went I was automatically put in his place and Eddie and I were re-united as partners. Indeed it was much more than just a tadger reunion. The new face was almost identical in height, shape and size with the South Shallow face and all the facemen with whom I had worked on the old district occupied stents on the new face, many of them in exactly the same positions as before. It was with soaring spirits that I resumed my old job as cable dragger, hearing the facemen moaning, 'Christ! Have we got to put up with him again?' and cursing me as only they knew how. After many wanderings I was home again!

CHAPTER TWELVE

The Tadger Man

FOR THE FOURTH and last time I watched autumn merge into winter on Cannock Chase, saw the days shorten and felt the air grow keener. With the return of the dark mornings the stars still shone as we descended the pit, while evening shadows were already clouding the sky when we returned to the surface at the end of the shift. Our warm breath puffed like white smoke on the frosty air as we raced for buses to take us back to the hostel where the lights gleamed cheerfully in the darkening haze.

Like the autumn leaves falling from the trees, the Bevin Boys continued to disappear till by mid November I, one of the youngest, found myself the last of my species on the new district. When Eddie was demobbed I succeeded him as tadger man, this time serving not just half a dozen facemen but nearly thirty on one of the busiest coal faces at Littleton Colliery. It was a proud moment for me when I collected my badge of office: a 'shiny' cap lamp such as the gaffers wore, which I clipped to my helmet, the current being supplied from a dry battery fastened to my belt. I was proud too when I joined all the other contract men in the pit canteen on Friday afternoon to collect my wages, which were twice as much as I had ever earned before.

For my mate I had a young Pole called Antoni who though he spoke English fairly well was mystified by the unorthodox pit vocabulary. I had to smile as I heard the facemen cussing him instead of me as he went slithering down the face with the cable, getting in everyone's way. I don't know who was the more fortunate, Antoni in not understanding what they were shouting at him or the facemen in not knowing what he was shouting in Polish back at them!

The D.Ps. at the hostel had suffered great hardship during the war and Antoni was no exception. Taken from Poland to Russia soon after the war started, he subsequently found his way to the Middle East where he joined up with Allied Forces. He had since learnt that his father had died though he did not know how. Of his mother he knew nothing, all his letters home being returned franked in Russian, 'Not Known.' He had little hope of returning to his own country again and was reconciled to starting life anew in England. In Poland he had been training to be an architect: now he was content to be a coal miner.

After I had been tadger man for a fortnight the facemen's original contract with the colliery expired and a new one was drawn up, as a result of which the tadger man ceased to be paid out of the facemen's bag but received a separate bag of his own from which he also had to pay his mate. This meant that I had become nothing less than a puffler though admittedly a very minor one. As a result of the new arrangement both Antoni and I received more money than we had previously been getting.

Each Monday morning I obtained from the check office a slip of paper on which I wrote the names of those who worked with me during the previous week and the number of shifts they and I had put in; the following Friday I collected the bag from the pay office and paid out accordingly. Of course if Antoni had put in a full week there was only his wages to find besides my own, but occasionally he missed a shift and the bag then had to be divided between three of us. As puffler I always made sure that any odd change went into my pocket!

It was a pity that this affluence was so late in arriving for after becoming a puffler I only remained at the colliery for three more weeks. On December 4th I received the following letter from the Ministry of Labour: 'Group No. 63. Dear Sir, The date of the release of the above Group Number will be 19th December, 1947, and if after that date you leave your present employment, the Department will not require you to take other employment in the coal mining industry.'

My reception of this letter was not what it might have been three years before. The truth was that the square peg had begun to fit in so comfortably that he did not particularly want to be uprooted. By this time my length of service in mining was twice that of any employment I had previously held; the miners were the people I knew best, and Cannock Chase, that abode of slag heaps, was the place with which I felt the strongest ties. I could see that it was going to take time to get adjusted back in my old job again.

Yet never did it occur to me, or to any other Bevin Boy I knew, to stay on in coal mining. This was not because of the underground life: we had got used to that by now. The reason lay in the fact that we had been forced into mining, with the result that escape had always been uppermost in our minds. At no time had we thought seriously of mining as a career though many of us were going home to less money than we were getting in the pits. From first to last coal mining had been a hateful job that had been thrust upon us. We were deliberately blind to its merits. All we wanted to do was get away from it.

Shortly after being notified of my impending release from the mines we received the following letter from the area office of the National Coal Board, headed 'To Ballottees, Optants and Volunteers.

'We thank you for your services to the Coal Mining Industry and appreciate very much the good work you have done. You have become somewhat experienced by now and we shall be sorry to lose your services. You came to us at a time of great stress and strain; the need for coal and the manpower is as great, if not greater, than when you came to us. We are, therefore, appealing to you to consider favourably remaining with us for a further temporary period to help us to tide over the immediate crisis. We can definitely promise, you will not prejudice your chance and opportunity for release, if you decide to remain and help us out in this Emergency. What we are really asking is for you to defer your application for release for a further temporary period'.

I read this letter with gratitude close to tears despite the fact that I was unable to answer the appeal it contained. The Bevin Boys had been in existence for four years and during that time had received no kind words and precious little encouragement. Until this letter came we had no indication whatever that our efforts had been either worthwhile or appreciated. For all we knew we were just as one M.P. described us: 'Not worth the trouble.'

I finished work at the colliery on December 19 but stayed on at the hostel until Christmas Eve. Each morning I lay in bed listening to the pit sirens echoing across the stirring moor: the whine of Valley, the boom of Cannock Wood and the distant wail of Littleton. It felt strange to lie there knowing that I would never again be racing up the hill on dark frosty mornings or stamping my feet to keep warm while waiting for the bus to arrive.

On Christmas Eve I packed my bags and got ready to leave for home. On the dormitory door the hostel housekeeper had pinned up the usual notice stating, 'Will all those going away for the Christmas holiday please state the date of departure and the date of return.' In the first column, opposite my bed number, I wrote 'December 24' and in the second, 'Never.'

It was getting dark as my train steamed out of the station loaded with festive passengers carrying holly and Christmas gifts. Forsaking the sing-song in my compartment I went into the corridor and stood in front of an open window, where I could feel the cold wind from off the moor beating in my face. With straining eyes I watched the familiar pitheads and chimneys hurry past in the semi-darkness and lingered on at the window till the last lights of Cannock Chase had vanished from sight.

INDEX

Pit Manager (Mr. Scurfield),   45, 81, 94
Pit Welfare Officer,   24, 30, 43

Regional Investigation Officer (Mr Genders),   44, 64, 76

Second World War,   2, 56
Shinwell, Ernest, Minister of Fuel & Power 1945-47,   66
"Simon", religious Bevin Boy,   43, 65, 75
South Shallow face, casualty, 30; construction and layout, 34-35; top
    road, 46; conditions on face, 53-54; breakdowns, 70-71; fault in
    seam, 80-81; effect of fault on drawing, 83-86, 95-97, 99-100, 104;
    cable dragging, 88-89; loading, 109; new face 97, 109, 111

Teeling, Flight-lieutenant, Conservative M.P. for Brighton, 1945,
    66-68

Under Manager,   29, 31, 34, 48-50, 81, 99

VE Day,   56-59
VJ Day,   63

Welfare Officer, training centre,   8-11
Wimblebury village,   25
Wimblebury Hostel, situation and appearance, 25; getting to work, 30;
    freeze-up, 42-43; residents' activities, 43-44, 73-74; expenses, 48;
    fatality, 75; flooding, 77-78; Irish workers, 91-92; Displaced Persons,
    109-111; farewell, 114-115; Winter of 1947, 92-95
Wolverhampton Express & Star,   77, 81